Disclaimer

All knowledge contained in this book is given for informational and educational purposes only. The author is not accountable for any results or outcomes from using this material. Constructive attempts have been made to provide accurate and practical information, but the author is not bound for the accuracy or use/misuse of this information

Bodybuilding for Beginners

The Scientific Approach to Muscle Hypertrophy:
Exercises and Programming to get Bigger and Stronger

Anthony W. Van Great

Summary

Introduction

Muscle hypertrophy is defined as an increase in muscle fiber size that occurs from training. When resistance training occurs, muscle fibers experience small tears or microtrauma. This damage causes protein degradation. After training, protein synthesis is also signaled. For hypertrophy to occur, protein synthesis must be greater than protein degradation. Factors such as hypertrophy may contribute to early strength increase. Traditionally, muscle hypertrophy is not predicted to occur until at least four weeks of strength training, which is the primary contributor to further increases in strength.

With adequate volume and duration, muscular adaptation occurs with almost all forms of resistance training; however, the type of contraction used in training affects the magnitude of muscle hypertrophy. Regular resistance training consists of combined concentric and eccentric contractions, but the primary emphasis of this form of exercise is on the concentric. When the eccentric portion is emphasized and properly stressed, eccentric contractions are more effective than concentric contractions for inducing muscle hypertrophy.

Eccentric contractions have also been shown to increase muscle protein synthesis to a greater extent than concentric contractions.

Resistance training in the upper body results in more significant hypertrophy compared to the lower body. A number of mechanisms may explain the more substantial hypertrophy in the upper-body than in lower-body muscles. Lower body muscles are frequently used in everyday living (i.e., walking, standing, etc.). Thus, these muscles may be habitually activated and have less of a training response than less often used upper body musculature.

When training to induce muscle hypertrophy, adequate training volume is needed to bring about significant adaptations. Factors that make up the amount of volume in a training program include:

The number of sets performed per session.

The number of repetitions performed per set.

The number of sessions performed per week.

Also, rest between sets and training sessions should be factored into the interplay of training prescription and muscle hypertrophy. The most significant gains in hypertrophy have been shown when utilizing multiple sets compared to single sets in exercise training.

Skeletal muscle hypertrophy increases a muscle's cross-sectional area (CSA). Skeletal muscle hypertrophy is governed by a host of hormones and growth factors, including satellite cells and testosterone.

An increase in muscle CSA is accomplished by:

• Increase in the size of myofibrils
• Incorporation of new contractile proteins into the Actin and Myosin filaments
• Incorporation of new proteins into the structural filaments
• Increase in Sarcoplasm
• Increase in the connective tissues surrounding the muscle, myofibrils, and muscle fibers.

An increase in CSA can be accomplished by two forms of hypertrophy: sarcomere and sarcoplasmic.

Sarcomere Hypertrophy—Incorporation of New Proteins in Actin and Myosin

Sarcomere hypertrophy is a muscle fiber enlargement due to increased sarcomere number and size. Sarcomeres, which contain the contractile proteins actin and myosin, are the "functional units" of myofibrils. Incorporating new contractile proteins into Actin and Myosin filaments increases a muscle fiber's size and ability to produce force, commonly referred to as strength. These new proteins must be created through the process of protein synthesis.

Sarcoplasmic Hypertrophy—Increase in Sarcoplasm and Connective Tissue

Sarcoplasmic hypertrophy increases the sarcoplasm (muscle fiber semifluid cytoplasm) and non-contractile proteins. The fiber's ability to produce force does not increase from sarcoplasmic hypertrophy. The emerging theory behind skeletal muscle hypertrophy is that a bout of exercise causes protein degradation or damage (microtrauma), which leads to a period of enhanced protein synthesis or supercompensation when the episode ceases. (Zatsiorsky, 1995). This increase in protein synthesis repairs the damage from the bout of exercise and makes the muscle stronger and more resistant to future damage.

Overview

Let's start with your muscles. They're composed of thousands of muscle fibers. These fibers come in different-sized bundles. Small muscle fibers end up in small bundles. Big fibers end up in big bundles. Small bundles are responsible for small, finite movements that don't generate much power, like writing your workouts with a pen. On the flip side, big muscle fibers like the glutes and hamstrings perform explosive, powerful movements such as sprints or squats. Through specific changes to your programming, we will incorporate the most significant number of muscle fibers to maximize the muscle-building training response. The smallest motor units fire up first when your muscles contract. When more force is needed, greater motor units are called to action. Imagine you're walking down the street, nice and relaxed, recruiting smaller units. Suddenly, a car swerves and is heading right for you.

That's when your body kicks into high gear, and you begin sprinting and jumping out of the way. This rapid, explosive action calls your larger motor units into play to generate explosive, high-speed movement compared to just strolling down the sidewalk. This increasing recruitment based on force demands is called the Size Principle, the recruitment of muscle units from smallest to largest. Regarding movement, your brain sends an electrical signal to the workout muscles to generate activity - the degree of motor unit recruitment depends on how strong the signal is. Here's something every gym goer can relate to. Imagine you're in the gym and watching someone lift a heavy weight for three or four fast, total-effort repetitions. Then, you watch another guy lift a moderate load, grinding through each rep without the same intensity.

In weight training, a heavier weight has more mass than a lighter weight. You'll generate more force by combining a heavy weight and accelerating each rep. Now there is a catch - you can't lift heavy during every workout.

Your nervous system, joints, and tissues would start screaming at you before too long. Luckily, there are two ways to maximize force when lifting: 1. Lift heavier weights 2. Lift lighter weights (or move your body) faster. That's why we combine heavy, moderate, and light weights to generate as much force as possible. Moving weights as fast and hard as possible will recruit more muscle fibers and maximize nervous system recruitment. This way, you'll get explosive and maximize your muscle-building potential with better muscle fiber recruitment.

Mechanisms of Hypertrophy

Increased muscle protein accretion following resistance exercise has been attributed to three primary mechanisms: mechanical tension, metabolic stress, and muscle damage. This chapter addresses each of these mechanisms and the theoretical rationale for its promotion of a hypertrophic response.

Mechanical Tension

Skeletal muscle is highly responsive to alterations in mechanical loading. Accordingly, many researchers have surmised that mechanical tension is the primary driving force in the hypertrophic response to regimented resistance training.

Mechanical tension alone has been shown to directly stimulate mTOR by activating the extracellular signal-regulated kinase/tuberous sclerosis complex 2 (ERK/ TSC2) pathway. It is theorized that these actions are mediated via the synthesis of the lipid second messenger phosphatidic acid by phospholipase D.

Research indicates that mechanosensors are sensitive to both the magnitude and temporal aspects of loading.

We will employ advanced techniques to maximize muscle growth, muscle damage, metabolic stress, and time under tension. According to The Mechanisms of Muscle Hypertrophy and Their Application to Resistance Training by Brad Schoenfeld, metabolic stress, mechanical tension, and muscular damage are the three primary methods of muscular hypertrophy.

The time you spend under tension from lifting a weight creates mechanical strain in the muscles; ergo, the more significant the time and resistance, the more powerful the mechanical tension. But tension alone won't signal maximum muscle growth. Tension, in addition to a full range of motion, induces a substantial hypertrophic response.

It sounds all-encompassing, but you need to lift heavy and apply longer-duration tension exercise through a full range of motion to maximize muscle growth.

Practical Example: A barbell Romanian deadlift uses a heavy load on the hamstrings with minimal cross bridging at the end range of motion, creating tons of mechanical stress for growth on your backside.

Muscular Damage: It's not uncommon to feel like your ass is super glued to the toilet the day after demolishing your legs. Your hobbles before your morning dump might be uncomfortable, but it isn't for naught. It indicates muscular damage that overloads your tissues past their current capacity. This comes through higher weight, higher volume, lower rest periods, or a combination of all three. Luckily, your pain isn't lost. The damage to muscle tissue creates a massive inflammatory response and migration of hypertrophy, promoting satellite cells to repair the tissues for massive growth.

Practical Example: It's simple yet vital: You must seek progressive overload in your workouts, or your body won't grow. Once you're doing this, the occasional drop-set is a super-dense method to create maximal muscular damage in minimal time. After your next upper body session, do this two times: • Elevate the feet and perform push-ups, stopping 2-3 reps shy of failure. • Without rest, drop to the floor and perform push-ups until technical failure— poor reps aren't worth it. • Then, elevate your hands on the bench and knock out as many push-ups as possible.

Metabolic Stress

Although the importance of mechanical tension in promoting muscle growth is indisputable, there is compelling evidence that other factors also play a role in the hypertrophic process. Metabolic stress is one such factor of particular relevance to exercise-induced anabolism. Simply stated, metabolic stress is an exercise-induced accumulation of metabolites, particularly lactate, inorganic phosphate, and H+. Several researchers have claimed that metabolite buildup may have an even more significant impact on muscle hypertrophy than high-force development, although other investigators dispute this assertion. Metabolic stress is maximized during exercise that relies heavily on anaerobic glycolysis for energy production. Anaerobic glycolysis is dominant during exercise lasting from about 30 - 45 mins.

Typical bodybuilding routines are intended to capitalize on the growth-promoting effects of metabolic stress at the expense of higher load intensities. These routines, which involve performing multiple sets of 8 to 12 repetitions per set with relatively short interset rest intervals, have increased metabolic stress much more than higher-intensity regimens typically employed by power lifters. It is well documented that despite regular training at moderate intensities of load, bodybuilders display hyper muscular physiques and levels of lean body mass at least as great as, if not greater than, those achieved by power lifters. Indeed, there is evidence that bodybuilding-type routines produce superior hypertrophic increases compared to higher-load powerlifting-style routines. However, findings are inconsistent across all trials when equating for volume load. Several factors are theorized to mediate hypertrophic adaptations from exercise-induced metabolic stress. These include increased fiber recruitment, myokine production alterations, cell swelling, reactive oxygen species (ROS) accumulation, and elevated systemic hormone production.

Fiber Recruitment

As discussed earlier, muscle fiber recruitment is carried out in an orderly fashion whereby low-threshold motor units, Increased fiber recruitment, Elevated hormonal response, Altered myokine production, Accumulation of ROS, Cellular swelling Metabolic stress are recruited first. Then higher-threshold motor units are progressively recruited to sustain muscle contraction depending on force demands. Although heavy loading activates the full spectrum of fiber types, research indicates that metabolic stress increases the recruitment of higher-threshold motor units even when lifting light loads. Studies show that recruitment thresholds decrease as fatigue increases during sustained submaximal exercise. Accordingly, activation of fast-twitch fibers is high, provided a set is carried out to the point of muscular failure.

Breakdown

If you've ever experienced a sleeve-splitting pump after the end of an arms workout, you've experienced the immediate effects of metabolic stress. When you lift hard to achieve a pump, you build up lactate, hydrogen ions, creatinine, and other metabolites while simultaneously preventing blood from escaping. With this stress, significant damage and anabolic signaling within your muscle fibers require repair to restore function. In other words, the high-rep sets that cause the pump and metabolic stress in the muscle signal that adaptation is needed to build muscle. As a result, recovery resources promote muscle fibers to recover and return stronger to respond to future stimuli. Some soreness is okay, but excessive damage may interfere with training frequency to the detriment of maximal hypertrophy.

Resistance Training Variables for Muscle Hypertrophy

Several research-based methods exist for examining the muscular response to mechanical stimuli. For example, synergist ablation of the gastrocnemius muscle results in the soleus and plantaris muscles being forced to carry out plantar flexion. The heightened load on these muscles results in increases in muscle cross-sectional area of 30% to 50% within several weeks post-surgery. Neuromuscular electrical stimulation also is frequently used to promote hypertrophy in animal models. This technique, which involves stimulating muscles with high-frequency electrical impulses (levels above 60 Hz), produces significant gains in muscle mass in just a few sessions. In humans, however, resistance training is the primary means of increasing muscle growth. Resistance training programs are a composite of program design variables that include volume, frequency, load, exercise selection, type of muscle action, rest interval length, repetition duration, exercise order, range of motion, and intensity of effort. These variables can be manipulated to stimulate the neuromuscular system, and they do so in different ways. Consistent with the SAID principle (specific adaptations to imposed demands), how such stimuli are applied influences phenotypic adaptations. This chapter provides an overview of each variable concerning how its manipulation affects the hypertrophic response to resistance training.

Volume

Training with a higher volume will increase metabolic damage, mechanical tension, and muscular damage in your training to boost your muscle-building capabilities. Disregarding other intensity-boosting methods, training with more volume creates enough overload to help you build muscle.

Volume refers to the amount of exercise performed over a certain period of time. Volume is often expressed as the number of repetitions completed in a resistance training bout (sets × repetitions). However, this value does not consider the amount of load lifted. Thus, a more appropriate term to reflect the total work completed is volume load, which is the product of sets × repetitions × load. Although an increase in training frequency can create the most significant increase in weekly volume load provided volume per session is kept static, an increase in the number of sets performed (and thus total repetitions) in a training bout can also substantially increase training volume. Research provides compelling evidence that higher-volume loads are necessary to maximize anabolism.

Multiset protocols favoring high volumes of resistance training optimize the hypertrophic response. To avoid overtraining, people should increase volume progressively throughout a training cycle and regularly integrate periods of reduced training volume to facilitate recovery.

Frequency

Training frequency pertains to the number of exercise sessions performed in a given time frame, generally a week. Perhaps more critical to hypertrophic outcomes, frequency also includes the number of times a muscle group is trained during seven days. Concerning hypertrophy training, the frequency can be varied to manipulate training volume. Neuromuscular factors limit how much volume can be incorporated into a single training session; beyond a given threshold, the quality of training begins to degrade.

Thus, distributing volume per muscle group over more frequent bouts can be an effective strategy for maintaining weekly volume with less fatigue per session. Hypertrophy-oriented routines generally involve a high volume of work per muscle group in a session but relatively infrequent training of each muscle group. To best carry out this strategy, people often follow a split body routine in which they perform multiple exercises for a specific muscle group in one training session. Compared to a full body routine, split routines allow total weekly training volume to be maintained or increased with fewer sets performed per training session and more significant recovery between sessions. Moreover, performing multiple exercises for a muscle group in the same bout heightens metabolic stress and thus may enhance anabolism. A survey of competitive male bodybuilders revealed that more than 2/3 trained each muscle group only once per week, and none reported working a muscle group more than twice weekly; every respondent reported using a split-body routine.

The extent of muscle damage also mitigates training frequency. Metabolically fatigued muscle fibers display a greater membrane permeability consequent to an increase in free calcium ions, leading to the activation of potassium channels and proteolytic enzymes. Performing a multiset, high-volume routine consistent with hypertrophy training protocols may thus require at least 48 to 72 hours of rest between workouts for the same muscle group to ensure adequate repair, recovery, and adaptation.

Modulating training frequency is an effective strategy for manipulating volume loads. There appears to be a benefit to higher training frequencies, at least over short-term training protocols. Thus, total-body routines represent an attractive option for maximizing training frequency for each muscle group. However, split routines allow for a greater volume of work per muscle group per session, potentially enhancing muscular adaptations via the dose-response relationship between volume and hypertrophy. A case can be made for periodizing frequency over time, altering the number of times a muscle group is trained weekly, depending on individual response. This can be accomplished by alternating total-body and split routines (e.g., progressing from 3 weekly sessions to 4 weekly sessions the next cycle and then culminating in a cycle of 6 weekly sessions). In this way, the lifter can maximize hypertrophy while reducing the potential for overtraining.

Load

The load lifted is widely considered one of the most critical factors in the hypertrophic response to resistance training. The load intensity refers to the percentage of 1RM employed in a given exercise. For example, if someone has a maximal bench press of 100 lb (45.5 kg) and performs a set with 80 lb (36.4 kg), then the intensity of load would be expressed as 80% of 1RM. Load intensity is often categorized into loading zones that correspond to repetition ranges. Typically, repetition ranges are classified as heavy (1- to 5RM), medium (6- to 12RM), and light (15+RM).

You can achieve hypertrophy in all loading zones. Low-load training emphasizes metabolic stress and promotes the most significant increases in local muscular endurance. In contrast, low-repetition, high-load training requires high mechanical tension and enhances the ability to lift heavier loads due to greater neural adaptations. There appears to be a fiber type-specific response in which heavy-load training produces more significant cross-sectional area increases in Type II fibers. Light loads have a preferential effect on type I hypertrophy. Thus, if the primary goal is maximizing hypertrophy without regard to strength-related factors, then training across a broad spectrum of repetition ranges (1 through 20+) is recommended to exploit all possible avenues for the complete development of the whole muscle. There is merit to focusing on a medium-repetition range (6- to 12RM) because it provides high levels of mechanical tension sufficient to stimulate the full array of fiber types while allowing for sufficient training volumes. Incorporating heavy loading (1- to 5RM) enhances strength, which ultimately enables the use of heavier loads during medium-repetition lifting. Additionally, you should include both light-load training to ensure the optimal development of Type I fibers and to improve muscle buffering capacity so that additional repetitions can be performed at a given medium intensity of load. On the other hand, if the goal is to promote hypertrophy to maximize strength, there appears to be little reason to employ loads less than approximately 70% of 1RM.

The compelling body of research indicates the presence of a strength–endurance continuum, in which lighter loads promote the ability to carry out submaximal resistive efforts at the expense of maximal force production. As expected when training with low loads, Type I fiber hypertrophy increases have limited transfer to strength-related improvements.

Exercise Selection

Architectural variances of individual muscles lend support to the notion of the need to adopt a multiplanar, multiangled approach to hypertrophy training using a variety of exercises. Moreover, evidence suggests that frequent exercise rotation is warranted to fully stimulate all fibers within a muscle and thus maximize the hypertrophic response. As mentioned in chapter 1, neural mechanisms are primarily responsible for increases in strength during the early stages of resistance training. Therefore, lifters in the initial training phase should focus on acquiring the necessary motor learning and control to perform exercise effectively. Simplification and repetition are essential in this context. Performing the same movements over and over ingrains motor patterns so that proper technique becomes second nature. Reducing degrees of freedom with machine-based training can be an effective means to enhance neural development for those who have difficulty with coordination. They can then progress to more complex variations in three-dimensional space. A variety of exercises should be employed throughout a periodized training program to maximize whole-body muscle hypertrophy. This should include the liberal use of free-form exercises (i.e., free weights and cables) that maximize the contribution of stabilizer muscles and machine-based movements that target specific muscles or portions thereof. Similarly, you should include both multi- and single-joint exercises in a hypertrophy-specific routine to maximize muscular growth.

Aerobic exercise can increase hypertrophy in sedentary people, primarily in type I muscle fibers. The extent of hypertrophic increases depends on the level of sedentarism; more significant gains are seen in the elderly than in the young. Intensities of ≥80% HRR are generally needed to elicit significant muscular growth. Although definitive evidence regarding the effects of aerobic volume on hypertrophy is lacking, research indicates that longer periods of sedentarism reduce the total weekly duration required to promote lean mass accretion. Concerning the modality of exercise, cycling appears to have the most significant hypertrophic benefit. However, the lack of studies on alternative modalities makes it challenging to draw firm conclusions on this variable. Significantly, muscular gains are limited to the early phases after initiating a regimented aerobic exercise program. Results plateau in a relatively short time, and evidence suggests that ongoing aerobic training can negatively impact Type II fiber hypertrophy.

Type of Muscle Action

Mechanosensors are sensitive to the magnitude and duration of stimulation and the type of imposed action. Chapter 1 discusses the three basic types of muscle actions are concentric, eccentric, and isometric. Mechanistically, there is a logical basis for speculation that eccentric actions produce the most significant anabolic response, and research often focuses on this type of muscle action. Eccentric strength is approximately 20% to 50% greater than concentric strength and allows heavier loading during exercise. Moreover, forces generated during eccentric training are 45% higher than those generated during concentric training and approximately double that of isometric contractions. The greater mechanical tension per active fiber is thought to be due to a reversal of the size principle of recruitment, which states that Type II fibers are selectively recruited at the expense of Type I fibers. Evidence for preferential Type II recruitment has been noted during plantar flexion, as has the release of the slow-twitch soleus muscle and the corresponding increase in activity of the gastrocnemius during the eccentric component of movement.

Hypertrophic advantages of eccentric exercise are also related to muscle damage. Although concentric and isometric exercises can induce muscle damage, the extent of damage is heightened during eccentric actions. This is believed to be due to greater force demands on fewer active fibers, which are prone to tear when attempting to resist lengthening. Because the weakest sarcomeres are located at different regions of each myofibril, it is hypothesized that the associated non uniform lengthening causes a shearing of myofibrils. This deforms membranes, particularly T-tubules, leading to a disturbance of calcium homeostasis that further damages muscle tissue by eliciting the release of the calcium-activated neutral proteases involved in degrading Z-line proteins.

Research investigating the effect of contraction modes on muscle protein synthesis has produced disparate results. Several studies have failed to demonstrate differences in mixed muscle or myofibrillar muscle protein synthesis after submaximal eccentric or concentric resistance exercise. Conversely, Moore and colleagues reported a more rapid rise in myofibrillar muscle protein synthesis following six sets of 10 work-matched maximal eccentric versus concentric knee extension repetitions. The discrepancies between findings suggest that although muscle protein synthesis is similar in all contraction modes during submaximal exercise, maximal eccentric actions enhance the accretion of muscle proteins.

Concentric and eccentric muscle actions appear to recruit muscle fibers in different orders, result in different signaling responses, and produce distinct morphological adaptations in muscle fibers and bundles. Therefore, you should incorporate both concentric and eccentric actions during training.

You should include both concentric and eccentric actions in hypertrophy-oriented training programs. These actions appear to complement each other from a growth standpoint. There is a lack of research investigating whether isometric movements provide an additive hypertrophic benefit when combined with dynamic concentric and eccentric training.

Rest Interval Length

The time between sets is referred to as the rest interval or rest period. Rest intervals can be classified into three broad categories: short (30 seconds or less), moderate (60 to 90 seconds), and long (3 minutes or more). Research demonstrates that rest interval length has distinct effects on the acute response to resistance training, and these responses have been hypothesized to affect chronic hypertrophic adaptations. Short rest intervals have been shown to increase metabolite accumulation markedly.

Long rest intervals provide a sustained ability to maintain mechanical tension throughout each successive set. Strength capacity is largely preserved over three sets with rest intervals of three minutes or more. However, metabolite accumulation diminishes with increasing rest between sets, particularly concerning lactic acid buildup.

Moderate rest periods provide an ideal compromise between metabolic stress and mechanical tension. A hypertrophy-type workout where people rested 90 seconds between sets showed significantly more significant increases in blood lactate concentration and reductions in pH compared to a strength-type workout with 5 minutes of rest between sets. Sixty-second rest intervals required a decrease of 5% to 10% in each successive set to maintain 8- to 12RM loads in resistance-trained subjects. Because moderate rest intervals induce a favorable metabolic environment without substantially compromising mechanical forces, a rest interval of 60 to 90 seconds is generally prescribed for maximizing hypertrophy.

Despite a theoretical concept that shorter rest intervals produce superior muscular adaptations, current research does not support such a contention. More extended interset rest periods may enhance hypertrophy by allowing for the maintenance of a more significant volume load. Thus, resistance training protocols should generally provide rest periods of at least 2 minutes to maximize the hypertrophic response.

That said, consistently training with shorter rest intervals has been shown to promote adaptations that ultimately facilitate the ability to sustain a significantly higher mean percentage of 1RM during training (384). These adaptations include increased capillary and mitochondrial density and an improved capacity to buffer hydrogen ions and shuttle them out of muscle, thereby minimizing performance decrements. Conceivably, this could allow volume maintenance with greater metabolic stress, ultimately leading to more significant muscle protein accretion. Therefore, it seems prudent to include training cycles that limit rest intervals to 60 to 90 seconds to take advantage of any additive effects of metabolic stress if they exist. In particular, high-repetition sets may benefit from short rest periods, given the reduced need to exert maximal force and the more significant potential for realizing the adaptations associated with improved buffering.

Although the results may seem compelling, you should note that cross-sectional muscle area was determined by anthropometric means (i.e., surface measurements), which can be quite unreliable and thus compromise accuracy. Further confounding matters is the small number of subjects (only 6 in each group) and the fact that subjects were not resistance trained.

Although rest periods of 60 to 90 seconds induce a favorable metabolic environment for achieving hypertrophy, research indicates that resting at least 2 minutes between sets provides a hypertrophic advantage compared to shorter rest periods because of the ability to maintain a more significant volume load.

Repetition Duration

Repetition duration represents the sum of a repetition's concentric, eccentric, and isometric components and is predicated on the tempo at which the repetition is performed. Tempo is often expressed as a three-digit arrangement in which the first number is the time (in seconds) to complete the concentric action, the second is the isometric transition phase between concentric and eccentric movements, and the third is the time to complete the eccentric action.

For example, a tempo of 2-0-3 would indicate a repetition taking 2 seconds on the concentric action, not pausing at the top of the movement, and then taking 3 seconds to perform the eccentric action. In the preceding example, the repetition duration would be 5 seconds. To a certain degree, you can volitionally manipulate tempo. The extent depends on two factors: the intensity of the load and the accumulated fatigue. Heavier loads take longer to lift; the closer the load is to the person's 1RM, the slower the concentric action will be, even when the intent is to move the weight as quickly as possible.

Moreover, the onset of fatigue causes velocity to decrease because of the inability of working fibers to maintain force output. The capacity to lift even very light loads is curtailed when repetitions approach failure. In one study, the first three concentric repetitions of a 5RM bench press took approximately 1.2 to 1.6 seconds, whereas the fourth and fifth repetitions took 2.5 to 3.3 seconds, respectively. These results were seen even though subjects attempted to lift explosively on all repetitions.

Current evidence suggests that little difference exists in muscle hypertrophy when training at isotonic repetition durations from 0.5 to 6 seconds. Training at very slow volitional durations (>10 seconds per repetition) appears to produce inferior increases in muscle growth.

Current evidence suggests little difference in muscle hypertrophy when training with isotonic repetition durations ranging from 0.5 to 6 seconds to muscular failure.

Thus, it would seem that you can use a relatively wide range of repetition durations if the primary goal is to maximize muscle growth. Research is limited on the topic, making it difficult to draw concrete conclusions. Concentric and eccentric tempos of 1 to 3 seconds can be viable options. On the other hand, training at very slow volitional durations (>10 seconds per repetition) appears to produce inferior increases in muscle growth. However, a lack of controlled studies makes it difficult to draw definitive conclusions. It is conceivable that combining different repetition durations could enhance the hypertrophic response to resistance training.

Exercise Order

Current resistance training guidelines prescribe placing large-muscle, multi-joint exercises early in a workout, and placing small-muscle, single-joint movements later. These recommendations are based on the premise that the performance of multi-joint exercises is impaired when the smaller secondary synergists are pre-fatigued by prior single-joint exercises. For example, the performance of the arm curl would fatigue the biceps brachii, thereby impeding the ability to overload the larger latissimus dorsi muscle during the subsequent performance of the lat pulldown. Despite wide acceptance that exercise order should proceed from large- to small-muscle groups, research is equivocal on the topic. Acute studies show that performance, as determined by the number of repetitions performed, is compromised in exercises performed toward the end of a session regardless of the size of the muscle trained. However, given the heavier loads used during multi-joint movements, the absolute magnitude of the decreases is generally greater in these exercises when performed after those involving small-muscle groups. Thus, volume load tends to be better preserved when large-muscle exercises are placed early in the training session.

Exercises included the bench press, lat pulldown, triceps extension, and arm curl. The training was carried out twice per week for 12 weeks. Muscle thickness of the triceps brachii increased only in the group that performed small-muscle group exercises first. However, differences in the thickness of the biceps were similar on an absolute basis. The same lab replicated this basic study design and similarly found more significant increases in triceps thickness when the

Evidence indicates a hypertrophic benefit for muscles worked first in a resistance training bout. Therefore, you should prioritize exercise to train lagging muscles earlier in the session. In this way, the person expends the most significant amount of energy and focuses on the sets of the most important. Whether the muscle group is large or small is of secondary concern.

The order of exercises progressed from small- to large-muscle groups. Although these findings might indicate a benefit to performing smaller-muscle-group exercises first, you should note that hypertrophy of the larger muscles was not assessed in either study. It is possible, if not likely, that whichever muscles were worked earlier in the session hypertrophied to a greater extent than those performed toward the end of the bout. This suggests a benefit to prioritizing exercise order so that lagging muscles are worked at the onset of a workout. It has been postulated that lower-body exercise should precede upper-body training. This is based on the hypothesis that lower-body exercise causes reduced blood flow that compromises the delivery of anabolic hormones to the upper-body musculature when performed after arm training.

Range of Motion

Basic principles of structural anatomy and kinesiology dictate that muscles contribute more significantly at different joint angles for given exercises. For example, there is evidence that the quadriceps muscles are differentially activated during knee extensions: the vastus lateralis is maximally activated during the first 60° of range of motion (ROM), whereas the vastus medialis is maximally activated during the final 60° of ROM. Similar findings have been reported during the arm curl: the short head appears to be more active in the latter phase of the movement (i.e., greater elbow flexion), whereas the long head is more involved in the early stage. When comparing partial and complete ROMs, the body of literature shows a clear hypertrophic benefit to training through a full ROM.

This has been displayed in upper and lower-body muscles using a variety of exercises. Pinto and colleagues showed that full ROM training of the elbow flexors (0 to 130° of flexion) produced more significant increases in muscle thickness compared to partial-range training (50 to 100° of flexion). The difference in effect size strongly favored the complete ROM condition (1.09 vs. 0.57, respectively), indicating that the magnitude of variance was meaningful. Similarly, McMahon and colleagues (482) showed that although knee extension at full ROM (0 to 90°) and partial ROM (0 to 50°) both increased quadriceps muscle cross-sectional area, the magnitude of hypertrophy was significantly greater at 75% of femur length in the full-range condition.

Maximal muscle development requires training through a complete ROM. Thus, full ROM movements should form the basis of a hypertrophy-oriented program. The stretched position appears particularly important to elicit hypertrophic gains. That said, integrating some partial-range movements may enhance hypertrophy.

Muscles are activated differentially throughout the range of motion. Complete ROM movements should therefore form the basis of a hypertrophy training program.

31

Intensity of Effort

The effort exerted during resistance training, often referred to as the intensity of effort, can influence exercise-induced hypertrophy. The intensity of effort is generally gauged by the proximity to muscular failure, defined as the point during a set at which muscles can no longer produce the force necessary for concentrically lifting a given load. Although the merits of training to failure are still a matter of debate, it is commonly believed that the practice is necessary to maximize the hypertrophic response. The primary rationale for training to failure is to maximize motor unit recruitment, which is a requisite for achieving maximal protein accretion across all fiber types. Evidence supporting this position is lacking, however. It has been demonstrated that fatiguing contractions result in a corresponding increase in surface EMG activity, presumably due to the increased contribution of high-threshold motor units to maintain force output as lower-threshold motor units fatigue. However, surface EMG is not necessarily specific to recruitment; increases in amplitude can be due to many other factors, including rate coding, synchronization, muscle fiber propagation velocity, and intracellular action potentials. The extent of motor unit activation likely depends on the magnitude of the load. During heavy-load training, the highest-threshold motor units are recruited almost immediately, whereas, during lighter-load training, the recruitment of these motor units is delayed.

Training to failure may also enhance hypertrophy by increasing metabolic stress. Training under anaerobic glycolysis conditions heightens the metabolites' buildup, which theoretically augments post-exercise anabolism. Moreover, the continued compression of vessels induces more significant acute hypoxia in the working muscles, which may further contribute to hypertrophic adaptations.

Multi-joint free-weight exercises like cleans and squats have a much greater nervous system and mechanical requirements than a triceps extension or biceps curl. Should the rest be the same?

No! Look at the muscles involved in a clean versus a biceps curl: quads, glutes, hamstrings, calves, traps, rectus abdominus, erector spinae versus the biceps and brachadorialis. The clean requires much larger muscles and neural requirements to execute the exercise. Major multi-joint exercises recruit more muscles and have greater neural requirements than isolation and single-joint exercises. The rest periods must match these requirements for a full recovery and optimal performance. Therefore, rest will be long enough during performance exercises to fully recover. Then, we'll keep things short on hypertrophy-based exercises to maximize growth. Training for muscle growth requires a well-rounded approach that emphasizes heavy weights/low reps (1-6), moderate weight with moderate reps (8-12), and the occasional higher rep sets (15+). Varied rest periods must be used, with 3-5 minutes, 45-90 seconds, and 0-30 seconds working best.

Role of Aerobic Training in Hypertrophy

It is commonly thought that aerobic endurance exercise produces little to no increase in muscle hypertrophy. This belief is consistent with evidence showing that aerobic-type exercise mediates catabolic pathways, whereas anaerobic exercise mediates anabolic pathways. Atherton and colleagues conducted pioneering work to elucidate differences in the intracellular signaling response between the two types of exercises. Using an ex vivo model, they electrically stimulated isolated rat muscles with either intermittent high-frequency bursts to simulate resistance-type training or continuous low-frequency activation to simulate aerobic-type training.

Post intervention analysis revealed that AMPK phosphorylation in the low-frequency condition increased approximately 2-fold immediately and 3 hours post stimulation, whereas phosphorylation was suppressed in the high-frequency condition over the same period. Conversely, phosphorylation of Akt was a mirror image of AMPK results: markedly greater phosphorylation was seen in the high-frequency condition. Recall from chapter 2 that AMPK acts as an energy sensor to turn on catabolic signaling cascades, whereas Akt promotes the intracellular signaling responses associated with anabolism. These findings led to the AMPK–Akt switch hypothesis, which states that aerobic and anaerobic exercise produce opposing signaling responses and thus are incompatible for optimizing muscular adaptations.

Intensity

The literature indicates that high intensities are necessary for achieving significant muscle growth from aerobic training. Decreases in muscle cross-sectional area of approximately 20% have been noted in both Type I and Type II fibers after 13 weeks of marathon run training. This shows that low-intensity exercise is not beneficial to hypertrophy and seems detrimental when carried out over long durations. Although the precise aerobic intensity threshold necessary to elicit hypertrophic adaptations seems to depend on the person's level of conditioning, current research suggests that at least some training should be carried out at a minimum of 80% of heart rate reserve (HRR). Training with brief high-intensity intervals (85% of V. O2 peak) interspersed with recovery was shown to increase thigh muscle cross-sectional area by 24% in middle-aged people with type 2 diabetes, indicating a potential dose-response relationship between hypertrophy and aerobic intensity.

Aerobic exercise can increase muscle hypertrophy in untrained people, but intensity needs to be high—likely 80% of HRR or more.

Volume and Frequency

Volume and frequency of aerobic training also seem to play a role in the hypertrophic response to aerobic exercise, a conclusion supported in the literature. Harber and colleagues found that untrained elderly men achieved levels of hypertrophy similar to those of their younger counterparts following 12 weeks of cycle ergometry training despite completing approximately half of the total mechanical workload. These findings indicate that more prolonged periods of sedentarism reduce the total volume necessary for increasing muscle mass. This gives credence to the hypothesis that reviving muscle lost over time is easier to achieve than increasing levels close to the baseline. Thus, you would seemingly require higher aerobic training volumes in untrained younger people to promote an adaptive response. The impact of volume may be at least in part frequency dependent.

Here, body composition changes in younger versus older men in response to a 6-month aerobic endurance protocol. Each session lasted 45 minutes, and training occurred five days per week. The intensity was progressively increased so that participants ultimately worked at 85% of heart rate reserve over the last two months of the study. Results showed that only the older men increased muscle mass; no muscular changes were seen in the younger men. The researchers noted that the attendance of the younger subjects was significantly less than that of their older counterparts, implying a hypertrophic benefit to greater aerobic training frequency. Notably, it is impossible to tease out the effects of frequency from volume in this study. Whether simply performing longer durations during a single session would confer similar benefits to spreading out frequency over a week is undetermined.

Mode What, if any, impact the modality of aerobic training has on hypertrophic adaptations is unclear. Most studies on the topic have involved cycling exercises, and most of these trials have shown increased muscle protein accretion with consistent training. Studies using non-cycling activities have produced mixed results.

The previously mentioned study by Schwartz and colleagues found increased muscle mass in elderly but not young male subjects following six months of a walk/jog/run protocol. In a study of elderly women, Sipila and Suominen showed that a combination of step aerobics and track walking at intensities up to 80% of HRR did not significantly increase cross-sectional muscle area after 18 weeks of training. These findings suggest that it may be more challenging to promote a hypertrophic effect from ambulatory aerobic exercise, perhaps because such activity is performed more often in daily life. Juries and colleagues reported no muscle cross-sectional area changes in elderly men and women following a 24-week stair climbing and kayaking-type aerobic exercise protocol performed with progressively increased intensity up to 85% of HRR.

Other Factors

Although the evidence indicates that aerobic training can induce growth in sedentary people, increases in whole-muscle hypertrophy do not necessarily reflect what is occurring at the fiber level. Consistent with its endurance-oriented nature, aerobic-type training appears to produce hypertrophic changes specific to Type I fibers. We found that Type I cross-sectional area increased by approximately 16% in a group of untrained elderly women following 12 weeks of cycle ergometry training; no change was noted in Type IIa fibers. A follow-up study employing a similar protocol in younger and older men showed that 12 weeks of cycle ergometry increased Type I fiber cross-sectional area by approximately 20%. Type IIa fiber diameter decreased in younger subjects, although not significantly, whereas that of the older subjects remained relatively constant. These findings imply that aerobic exercise may have a detrimental effect on hypertrophy of the faster fiber types. However, other studies show beneficial effects of aerobic training on Type II fiber cross-sectional area in older and younger subjects. The cause of the discrepancies in findings between studies is not clear.

Aerobic exercise can increase hypertrophy in sedentary people, primarily in type I muscle fibers. The extent of hypertrophic increases depends on the level of sedentarism; more significant gains are seen in the elderly than in the young. Intensities of $\geq 80\%$ HRR are generally needed to elicit significant muscular growth. Although definitive evidence regarding the effects of aerobic volume on hypertrophy is lacking, research indicates that longer periods of sedentarism reduce the total weekly duration required to promote lean mass accretion. Concerning the exercise modality, cycling appears to have the greatest hypertrophic benefit. However, the lack of studies on alternative modalities makes it challenging to draw firm conclusions on this variable. Significantly, muscular gains are limited to the early phases after initiating a regimented aerobic exercise program. Results plateau in a relatively short time, and evidence suggests that continuous aerobic training can negatively impact Type II fiber

Hypertrophy

Interestingly, only the high-intensity condition showed sustained muscle protein synthesis elevations at 24 to 28 hours post exercise recovery. Based on these acute results, it would seem that sarcoplasmic proteins account for a considerable portion of aerobic-induced hypertrophic adaptations. Given the evidence that the growth of a given muscle fiber is achieved at the expense of its aerobic endurance capacity, the accretion of mitochondrial proteins seems to hurt the ability to maximize gains in contractile proteins. An important limitation of current research is that the time course of hypertrophic adaptations during aerobic training has not been well investigated. In sedentary people, virtually any training stimulus—including aerobic exercise—is sufficient to overload muscle. This necessarily results in an adaptive response that promotes tissue remodeling. However, the intensity of aerobic training is not enough to progressively overload muscle in a manner that promotes further adaptations over time. Thus, it stands to reason that the body would quickly plateau after an initial increase in muscle size.

Concurrent Training

Aerobic exercise is often performed with resistance training for accelerating fat loss, enhancing sports performance, or both. This strategy, called concurrent training, has been shown to affect weight management positively. However, evidence suggests that adding aerobic exercise to a regimented resistance training program may compromise muscle growth. Adverse hypertrophic effects from concurrent training have been attributed to a phenomenon known as chronic interference, the hypothesis for which alleges that trained muscle cannot simultaneously adapt optimally morphologically or metabolically to both strength and aerobic endurance training. Like the AMPK–Akt switch hypothesis, the chronic interference hypothesis states that these competing adaptations produce divergent intracellular signaling responses that mitigate muscular gains. Despite the logical basis for the chronic interference theory, the phenomenon's effect on humans when performing traditional training protocols is unclear. Although some studies show that combining aerobic and resistance exercise impedes anabolic signaling, others have failed to note any negative consequences.

Another potential issue with concurrent training is an increased potential for overtraining. When training volume or intensity exceeds the body's ability to recover, physiological systems are disrupted. The stress of adding aerobic exercise to an intense hypertrophy-oriented resistance training program can overtax recuperative abilities, leading to an over trained state. The interference effects of aerobic exercise associated with overtraining may be mediated by a catabolic hormonal environment and chronic muscle glycogen depletion.

Long-term training studies investigating muscular adaptations to concurrent training have produced conflicting findings. Evidence suggests that aerobic exercise blunts the hypertrophic response to resistance training when considering the body of literature.

A meta-analysis by Wilson and colleagues revealed that those who solely lifted weights reduced effect size for muscular gains by almost 50% when they added aerobic endurance training to the mix. However, multiple factors ultimately determine how and to what extent aerobic training influences the adaptations associated with resistance training. In particular, manipulating aerobic exercise intensity, volume and frequency, mode, and scheduling is paramount in creating the response. The following sections provide an overview of these variables and their reputed effects on resistance training-induced hypertrophy.

Evidence suggests that, over time, aerobic exercise blunts the hypertrophic response to resistance training.

Volume and Frequency

Volume may significantly impact the hypertrophic interference associated with concurrent training, potentially related to overtraining symptoms induced by a catabolic hormonal environment and chronic muscle glycogen depletion. This contention is supported by research showing attenuations in maximal strength with frequencies of more than three sessions per week but not less than two sessions per week. Pooled data from Wilson and colleagues revealed a significant negative correlation between muscle hypertrophy and aerobic exercise volume (duration and frequency) during concurrent training.

Mode

Although aerobic exercise can be carried out using a variety of modalities, running and cycling have primarily been studied in the context of concurrent training. The meta-analysis by Wilson and colleagues revealed that running had a particularly negative effect on the hypertrophic adaptations associated with resistance training, whereas cycling did not appear to cause a significant detriment. The authors speculated that running-related impairments on muscle growth could be related to excessive muscle damage caused by its high eccentric component. Conceivably, this could inhibit recuperative abilities and thus blunt the post exercise adaptive response. Alternatively, they proposed that cycling has more remarkable biomechanical similarities to multi-joint free-weight exercise compared to running and may have provided a more significant transfer of training. Counter intuitively, high-intensity aerobic cycling negatively affected strength to a greater degree than high-intensity treadmill running when performed immediately before a resistance training bout. Over time, this would likely have a detrimental impact on hypertrophy due to chronic reductions in mechanical tension.

Factors in Maximal Hypertrophic Development

Many population-specific factors affect skeletal muscle mass and the hypertrophic response to resistance exercise. Genetics, age, sex, and training experience are of particular note in this regard. This chapter provides an overview of these factors and their effects on the ability to increase muscle size.

Genetics

A person's genotype and phenotype determine a theoretical upper limit to muscle fiber size. Genotype can be broadly defined as the genetic makeup of an organism; phenotype refers to how genotypes are expressed. In short, genetically coded information (genotype) is interpreted by the body's cellular machinery to produce the physical properties of the muscle (phenotype). Concerning hypertrophy, someone may have the genetic makeup to become an elite bodybuilder, for example. Still, if they never engage in a regimented resistance training program, that genotype will not be expressed to bring about a championship-caliber physique. The manifestation of muscle genotype and phenotype has been extensively researched. Twin studies show that up to 90% of the variance in baseline muscle mass is hereditary, and stark inter-individual hypertrophic differences are seen in response to a resistance training program.

A variety of genetic factors influence hypertrophic potential and this influence declines with advancing age.

Age

The aging process is associated with alterations in both muscle quantity and quality. Human muscle mass reaches peak levels between the ages of 20 and 40. After that, the body loses approximately 0.5% of its muscle mass per year during the fourth decade of life, increasing to 1% to 2% annually after age 50 and then accelerating to 3% annually after age 60. This age-related loss of muscle tissue has been termed sarcopenia. Sedentary people show more prominent rates of decline than active people, although leisure-time physical activity has only minor effects on tempering muscle loss. Sarcopenic changes have been attributed to reduced basal, post absorptive myofibrillar muscle protein synthesis, elevated proteolysis, or both. Still, more recent findings suggest that basal skeletal muscle net protein balance is not compromised with aging in healthy people.

Alternatively, it has been postulated that chronic systemic inflammation may compromise muscle protein metabolism in frail elderly. Various disease states and lifestyle factors are known to exacerbate the rate of muscle wasting with age. Sarcopenia is characterized not only by fiber atrophy but also by widened sarcoplasmic spaces and Z-band and myofibrillar disruption.

After age 40, the body loses progressively more muscle mass per year. Regular resistance training can reduce this loss. Although the elderly have a diminished hypertrophic response, they can gain muscle mass; however, a more significant weekly training dose appears necessary to maintain the gains.

Sex

Substantial sex-based differences exist in the maintenance and hypertrophy of skeletal muscle tissue. On average, women have less muscle mass than men from an absolute and relative standpoint. These discrepancies become evident during puberty and persist through old age. It is believed that hormonal variances between the sexes highly influence sexual dimorphism. Testosterone levels in men are approximately ten times higher than those in women. As discussed in chapter 1, testosterone is a highly anabolic hormone that exerts its actions by increasing myofibrillar protein synthesis and decreasing muscle protein breakdown. Theoretically, low circulating testosterone levels in women would substantially reduce the potential to increase muscle mass. However, attenuations in anabolism from a lack of testosterone appear to be partially offset by higher estrogen levels. The anabolic effects of estrogen are attributed to reductions in muscle protein breakdown, a hypothesis supported by research showing that hormone replacement therapy counteracts the up-regulation of the ubiquitin-proteasome system in menopausal women. There also is evidence that estrogen positively modulates myogenic gene expression following resistance training, indicating a potential role in enhancing sensitivity to anabolic stimuli. On a relative basis, men and women experience similar increases in muscle hypertrophy following regimented resistance training. However, you must understand these results in the context that women start with less muscle mass at baseline, thus biasing increases in their favor. From an absolute standpoint, hypertrophic gains are significantly greater in men than in women.

Although men and women experience similar relative increases in muscle hypertrophy following controlled resistance training, from an absolute standpoint, men can obtain significantly more significant total gains, which is attributed mainly to their higher testosterone levels.

Aging appears to have a particularly detrimental effect on muscle mass in women. Despite higher resting protein synthetic rates in the postmenopausal period, elderly women experience accelerated muscle loss resulting from increased rates of proteolysis, a phenomenon partly attributed to decreased estrogen production. Moreover, the anabolic response to protein feeding is blunted to a greater degree in older women. In addition, the hypertrophic response to resistance training is impaired in elderly women, as are post exercise elevations in muscle protein synthesis. Taken together, these findings indicate that postmenopausal reductions in estrogen in women have a more detrimental impact on muscle mass than decreased testosterone levels associated with aging in men. Despite these obstacles, elderly women can significantly increase fundamental muscle mass with regimented resistance exercises. Training-induced increases in hypertrophy have been correlated with reductions in primary inflammatory markers.

Training Status

The vast majority of resistance training studies are carried out on untrained people. This is generally a function of convenience because the pool of untrained subjects is larger than that of resistance-trained subjects. However, the hypertrophic response of trained subjects is substantially different than that of their untrained counterparts, thereby limiting the generalizability of such studies outside the initial stages of training. Differences in the hypertrophic potential between trained and untrained people can be attributed to the ceiling effect or window of adaptation. During the initial stages of training, the neuromuscular system is deconditioned and responds to virtually any stimulus because the ceiling for growth is high. Even steady-state cardiorespiratory exercise has been shown to produce hypertrophic increases in previously sedentary people. As people become resistance trained and move closer to their genetic ceiling, it becomes progressively more challenging to increase muscular size (i.e., the window of adaptation becomes smaller).

Theoretically, an excess of muscle mass would be energetically and kinetically inefficient; thus, the human body limits the amount of lean tissue it can gain. In support of this hypothesis, research shows that the extent of hypertrophic gains is relatively small (~3% to 7%) in highly competitive bodybuilders over five months of resistance training, suggesting these people are at the upper limits of their genetic ceilings. Alterations in anabolic intracellular signaling have been demonstrated between trained and untrained subjects in animal and human models. Ogasawara and colleagues exposed male rats to maximal isometric contractions via percutaneous electrical stimulation of the gastrocnemius muscle every other day for either one bout, 12 bouts, or 18 bouts. Those in a detraining group performed 12 bouts, detrained for 12 days, and then were subjected to an additional exercise session prior to being sacrificed.

Phosphorylation ribosomal proteins were elevated in the group that performed one bout, but repeated exercise bouts suppressed phosphorylation levels. This indicates that anabolic signaling becomes desensitized to resistance training when performed consistently over time.

As people become resistance trained and move closer to their genetic ceiling, increasing muscular size becomes progressively more challenging. Meaningful hypertrophic responses can be gained by precise manipulation of program variables, including brief strategic periods of de-loading to restore the anabolic responsiveness of trained muscle.

GETTING STARTED FOR A BEGINNER

Before we proceed, let's clear up a misconception about bodybuilding that has existed for years. The truth is: Bodybuilding, done correctly, does not make you stiff or muscle-bound. In years past, coaches often discouraged athletes from lifting weights. They feared that large muscles would make the athletes bulky and slow instead of nimble and quick. Some players recognized the value of weight training but often had to lift weights without their coach's knowledge. Gradually, the benefits of muscle development have won coaches over in virtually every sport. Take baseball, for instance. Many of today's best hitters have physiques that rival many bodybuilders. Decades ago, the best players often had thin, unimpressive builds. The word gradually spread in baseball and other sports that proper weight lifting can improve—instead of inhibiting—flexibility and speed.

In addition, greater strength can increase stamina and durability. Among non-athletes, however, there remain some people who think that bodybuilders, with all their mass, must be so muscle-bound that they can't even reach down to tie their shoes. Wrong! They should watch Flex Wheeler, one of today's top bodybuilders, as he does full splits onstage. That's right—full splits, with one leg extended straight in front and the other straight behind as he lowers himself to the floor. We usually associate splits with tiny, pre-teen gymnasts blessed with incredible flexibility. Wheeler, by contrast, stands over six feet tall and weighs about 250 pounds in contest shape. His flexibility matches up with anybody. So, to those who say, "I don't want to start lifting weights because I might get too big," we say, "Find another excuse." Women, in particular, often fear that they'll become big and masculine if they begin serious weight training. They don't want to look like a female version of Arnold Schwarzenegger.

There is very little chance that a woman would ever resemble a male bodybuilder, even if she tried. Some women, it is true, have exceeded the bounds of femininity with their massive development. Still, these are exceptions, not rules, and many have relied on potentially dangerous drugs to boost their growth. Women lack the genetic makeup to achieve the extreme muscularity of men. Most women embrace bodybuilding to tone, shape and firm their bodies—not to see how big they can make their muscles. Women often get as much satisfaction from bodybuilding as men, but for different reasons. They find that it helps them manage their weight far better than yo-yo dieting and helps them achieve a lean, graceful physique.

There are right ways and wrong ways to begin bodybuilding. If you don't learn the proper weightlifting form, you can seriously injure your back, knees, or shoulders—virtually any part of your body. It takes time to become comfortable handling barbells and dumbbells (free weights). The sophisticated weight machines in today's gyms can be easier to use, but they, like free weights, can be dangerous if misused. Here's the best advice: start slowly. Use lightweight at first until you master the correct lifting technique. Never bend from the waist and lift with your back. If you do, you risk back strain and perhaps chronic back trouble. Instead, bend at your knees and slowly lower yourself to the floor, keeping your back straight. Then grab the weight and gradually stand up. Now you're ready to begin your exercise. Always lift in a smooth, controlled, rhythmic manner. Once you start, never make quick, jerky movements with a barbell or dumbbell. For instance, don't rock your body back and forth to try to lift a heavy weight. Don't try to impress others in the gym by showing how much weight you can lift. The form is far more critical. If you try to lift too much weight, your form will suffer, and so will your results. Think of bodybuilding as a marathon, not a sprint.

Look for gradual progress, not overnight miracles. The key to successful bodybuilding is isolating specific muscles and working them to exhaustion. The muscles then recover and, over time, become stronger and larger. Different weightlifting exercises are designed to target different muscles. If you use your whole body during an exercise instead, you spread out the effort and fail to pinpoint one particular muscle. As a result, that muscle gets very little benefit. It is far better to have several short workouts a week than one killer session that lasts hours and hours. A long workout might leave you so sore and exhausted that you must take time off to recover.

Here's another vital point to consider as you begin bodybuilding: Genetics plays a crucial role in your ability to build a muscular physique. Anyone who trains properly over time can make impressive gains—but not everyone can become a champion bodybuilder. It may seem unfair, but some people are born with a genetic makeup that lends itself to great muscularity. These people often train less than others yet achieve far greater results. You need to assess your body before you begin serious training realistically. You don't have to be naturally athletic to achieve bodybuilding success, but it helps. Experts have identified three basic body types. Everyone fits more or less into one of these categories. Try to determine which body type best describes your frame.

• Ectomorphs naturally have a thin, wiry build with little body fat. They tend to have small muscles.

• Endomorphs are large and "doughy" by nature, with plenty of fat. They are stronger than ectomorphs, but their muscles aren't developed or defined.

• Mesomorphs are neither skinny nor fat. They have an attractive natural physique, and their muscles respond quickly to training. Most outstanding bodybuilders fit into this category.

Remember that no one is entirely an ectomorph, an endomorph, or a mesomorph. Most of us have all three characteristics, although one type is dominant. Why is this important? Your body type dictates the training you should do— and often predicts the results you'll achieve. For instance, an ectomorph doesn't need to worry about losing fat to build an incredible physique, but they may struggle to develop and maintain large muscles. Don't get discouraged if you're an ectomorph. Some great bodybuilders have had this body type. Just understand that you may have to work harder to achieve your goals if you're thin by nature. Endomorphs, on the other hand, may always fight a weight problem. However, their natural bulk can be an asset, too. If they train correctly, they can awaken the muscles hidden beneath the fat and develop these muscles to great size. Many outstanding bodybuilders have been endomorphs. Mesomorphs are the lucky ones. They typically don't have to fight the battle of the bulge or work out furiously to maintain their muscular development. They can make rapid, impressive gains as soon as they begin serious training. Some top bodybuilders who are mesomorphs have won major titles within a few years of taking up the sport. However, don't get the idea that mesomorphs get a free ride.

Just like ectomorphs and endomorphs, they have to work out intensely week after week, month after month, year after year, to achieve greatness. It's impossible to overemphasize the role of dedication and intensity in bodybuilding. These qualities are just as important—if not more so—than your body type. In any endeavor, people with enough "want to" can surpass people with more natural ability. The same is true for bodybuilding. If you commit to a regular workout regimen—and train hard—you're assured of achieving respectable results. Intensity is critical. Some people love to go to the gym but don't work out hard. They like to talk, look in the mirror, or stand by the water fountain. If they spend an hour in the gym, they think they've had a great workout. Not true. Time in the gym doesn't necessarily equal results. Yes, some elite bodybuilders are known for spending four or five hours at a time working out, but that's generally not necessary.

Some great bodybuilders spend only an hour or two at a time in the gym, but they know how to maximize every minute. They don't waste time with nonsense.

Because of differences in training intensity, it's hard to say how long you should work out. Thirty minutes? Forty-five minutes? An hour? Generally, you'll make good progress if you start with a 45-minute workout three times a week. That will let you work all the major muscle groups Some people, often because of their body type, see results far more quickly than others. They're "easy gainers." By starting with shorter workouts, you'll also find out if you enjoy weight lifting. You won't become a great bodybuilder if you constantly have to force yourself to go to the gym. It may seem obvious, but you've got to like— or even love—weight training to sculpt a fantastic physique. Bodybuilders who have left their mark on the sport couldn't stay away from the gym. For them, the problem was often overtraining—working out so often that they didn't give their bodies time to recover. We'll discuss overtraining later in the book, but it's a significant problem for some people. You must remember that proper rest and recovery are critical to progress. For now, don't worry about overtraining. Focus on learning to lift properly and becoming comfortable with weights. If overtraining ever becomes an issue, you can deal with it then.

UNDERSTANDING DIET AND NUTRITION

When most people think about bodybuilding, they think of weight training as the most significant component, but diet is almost as vital in getting the desired physique. If you eat junk food, no amount of weight lifting will develop a top-notch body. We've learned a lot about the importance of nutrition in recent years. Sure, everyone makes mistakes and eats things they shouldn't, and bodybuilders are no exception. It's not that you can never cheat again if you want to be a successful bodybuilder, but watching what you eat must be a big part of your training. Just as you need to understand your muscles and how they work, you need to be aware of the basics of nutrition: protein, carbohydrates ("carbs"), and fat. Each plays a critical role in your diet. What do we mean by "diet"? To many people, "diet" means counting calories and starving themselves. That form of dieting usually is counterproductive. You may limit calories enough to lose weight for a short while, but you almost invariably gain it back. In bodybuilding, "diet" means your overall eating habits. To add muscle, you have to consume a lot of calories. You can't get huge by eating like a bird. "Train big, eat big, sleep big"— that's the advice some people give. Naturally, what you eat is critical.

For instance, you won't achieve excellent muscle definition if you take in too much fat. Bodybuilders face the delicate balance of eating enough to gain muscle mass but keeping their body fat percentage low enough for definition (about 8% to 11% for men and 7% to 9% for women). There's no single perfect diet for everyone, just as there's no perfect weight training regimen for everyone. As you learn about nutrition, you'll be able to craft an eating plan that helps you achieve your fitness objectives. Knowledge is power—both in weight lifting and in eating. The two go hand in hand. In the past, most people considered three square meals a day as the best diet. Nutritionists have learned that eating fewer, smaller meals daily is far better. Our bodies need to be fed often, but they don't need to be overwhelmed by large quantities.

For instance, eating a big meal of meat, vegetables, bread, and dessert an hour or so before bed is not good. You won't expend those calories since you're sleeping, and they'll turn into fat. Bodybuilders typically consume most of their calories during the day, when they are more active, rather than at night. They frequently prepare food ahead of time and bring it with them so they can stick to their diet. You should follow suit. Preparing meals ahead of time ensures that you have plenty of nutritious food on hand and that you are not tempted to eat junk food.

Meal tips you should not ignore

You Have to Eat.

Suppose you want to be lean and have a shredded six-pack you have to eat. Starving yourself will result in a loss of muscle, a screwed-up metabolism, and a skeletal appearance. Eating will provide your body with everything it needs to burn fat, keep your metabolism working, feed your muscles, and ultimately get shredded – but remember, you need to eat the right foods. You won't be able to get shredded by eating whatever you want unless you're a freak of nature or on steroids. You should base your diet on whole foods and avoid processed/manufactured foods. (A shopping list of foods can be found in your gift.) Whole foods are anything that isn't packed with additives and comes from a factory.

Sure, the packet of cooked chicken at the grocery store boasts 30g of protein. Still, a closer look at the nutritional information reveals a long list of additives that will prevent you from ever becoming truly lean. Conversely, eating whole-natural foods (nuts, grass-fed beef, organic chicken, eggs, beans, legumes, etc.) will give your body the nutrients required to burn the stubborn fat hiding your abs. Going 100% natural can be challenging and is not essential. Instead, you should aim for 80% whole foods.

Eat Organic

Fruits and vegetables are high in vitamins and minerals that your body requires to build muscle and manage every function. We can eat as many of these as we like with any diet because they are only beneficial to us! These organic products are easy to purchase and incorporate into our regular diets. Hopefully, they are something you already consume a lot of, so the transition won't be too tricky! Consume plenty of protein!

It's essential to look at our food source because many animals are fed unhealthy grains and antibiotics to cope with their awful living environments. Hence, the result is something not so pleasant.
Sticking with organic products can help to negate this because these animals are raised as nature intended.

Eliminating grains and dairy from your diet can have a disadvantageous impact on your health. With this, you merely need to get the balance right. Eat fresh, eat natural, eat whole, and you're sure to see remarkable results in your fitness and general health.

Cut Out Junk

According to the Centers for Disease Control and Prevention, an estimated 70% of all individuals in the United States are overweight or obese due to poor diet. This is due to the amount of fat and sugar in our diets, which include many ostensibly diet foods. To acquire the right, healthy body, you must read all the labels on everything you eat. You'll sometimes want to know exactly what you're putting into your body.

Don't Be Afraid of Fat

It may sound counterintuitive, but eating fat aids with weight loss. Your body needs fat to function; it's a necessary building component, and eating enough of it will help you attain your goals faster. Extra-virgin olive oil, steak, beef, chicken thighs, and avocado are the primary sources of fat you should consume. If you severely restrict your fat intake, your body will go into "survival mode," refusing to let go of its existing fat stores because it will react as if no more is going to be added. Avoid this by including healthy dietary fats in your diet.

Let's look at the three primary macronutrients: protein, carbohydrates, and fat.

PROTEIN

Protein is the most critical macronutrient for bodybuilders. Protein is crucial for muscle tissue growth, maintenance, and repair, which is why top bodybuilders regularly monitor their protein consumption. A bodybuilder requires twice as much protein as the average individual. Animal proteins such as eggs, fish, chicken, meat, and dairy products are the most acceptable protein sources. Plant proteins, found in foods such as rice, beans, corn, peas, and almonds, are not as easily absorbed by the body as animal proteins. Vegetarians make up a small percentage of professional bodybuilders. Meat is a complete protein, which means it contains all amino acids, which are the building blocks of protein. By contrast, vegetables, nuts, and fruits lack one or more of the essential amino acids and are considered incomplete proteins. Therefore, a person would have to eat a wide range and larger amounts of plant protein foods to get the same benefit that a small serving of meat would provide.

Being shredded is not just about losing body fat. You also need to have a substantial amount of muscle. Lean muscle burns fat. The more muscle you have, the more fat you burn, and the building block of muscle is protein.

When you are on the quest to reveal your abs, you will be in a calorie deficit (expending more calories than you take in), and when in a deficit, protein will carry out the following functions:
- Keep you feeling fuller longer as protein aids satiety and prevents hunger.
- Prevent muscle breakdown from calorie reduction.

Some nutritional experts say it's possible to eat too much protein and that excessive amounts can damage the liver and kidneys. Most top bodybuilders, however, believe it's safe— and necessary—to consume a lot of protein. The U.S. government recommends that the average person eat 0.36 grams of protein daily for each pound of body weight. For a 180-pound man, that's about 65 grams of protein per day.

If that person is a bodybuilder, conventional bodybuilding wisdom says that they should consume twice because it's believed that too little protein will lead to greater muscle soreness and fatigue after a workout.

Protein Supplements

Protein, unlike some nutrients, cannot be stored in the body. Instead, you must consume it continuously to be useful—yet another reason to eat frequently. Most bodybuilders take protein supplements to get enough protein, usually in powder form and mixed with juice, milk, or water. Most modern supplements contain little or no fat and taste significantly better than previous supplements. You don't have to hold your nose to drink a protein shake any longer. Protein supplements are useful since they are considerably more straightforward to prepare and consume than a full meal while still providing the majority of the essential nutrients. Cost, however, can be a significant factor, so be sure to compare prices on supplements. Some are extraordinarily expensive, while other, much cheaper supplements are just as beneficial. Protein supplements are usually from whey, egg whites, soy, or milk. There are differing views on which protein source is best. Some medical researchers, for instance, say that soy protein can help lower cholesterol in some people. If you have high cholesterol, you should take a soy-based supplement. Powdered milk is a simple, low-cost protein supplement that has been around for a long time. You can use it with water, milk, or yogurt to make a cheap protein supplement. It won't deliver all of the benefits of today's high-tech supplements, which are loaded with vitamins and minerals, but it will provide high-quality protein to help with muscle growth.

CARBOHYDRATES

Carbohydrates are the body's primary source of energy. However, protein and fat supply some energy. About 50% of a bodybuilder's calories should come from carbohydrates. Carbs fall into two categories: simple and complex. Simple carbs provide a quick burst of energy. When they are digested, they turn into glucose, a significant source of energy that you can burn rapidly. Candy is one example of a simple carb; fruit is another healthier type. Complex carbs, on the other hand, fuel the body over a longer period of time. Everyone requires two kinds of carbohydrates, but bodybuilders should choose complex carbohydrates because they give a more consistent supply of energy throughout the day. Complex carbohydrates are further subdivided into fibrous and starchy carbs. Asparagus, green beans, broccoli, lettuce, mushrooms, spinach, and zucchini are all excellent sources of fiber carbohydrates. Red beans, corn, oats, peas, pasta, potatoes, rice, and tomatoes are examples of starchy carb sources. Green vegetables and carbohydrates, such as lentils, provide significant health benefits, making them vital for getting shredded. Eating extra fiber has been shown to help you control weight swings, reduce weight faster, support a healthy heart, and boost fullness after a meal. Consume some greens and fiber at each meal. As you read through the recipes in this book, you'll note that they're used in a lot of them.

Low-Carb Diets

People in today's weight-conscious world are continuously looking for a diet that would result in rapid weight loss. Low-carb diets have grown highly fashionable in recent years. They can be highly effective for some people. This is how they work: When fewer carbs are available, the body burns more fat for energy, resulting in weight reduction. A low-carb diet may appear attractive, but it can have major consequences. For starters, reducing your carbohydrate intake might cause fatigue and dehydration. Second, as your body burns fat, it may also burn muscle. In other words, you can lose some of the muscle mass you've worked so hard to attain. Third, carbohydrates are necessary for the proper functioning of your brain, heart, and vital organs. As you can see, carbs are critical to a person's well-being. Be very careful with eating plans that recommend low amounts of carbohydrates.

Carbohydrate Supplements

Because it can be challenging to get enough quality carbs in a regular diet, carb supplements are popular with many of today's top bodybuilders. Since an intense workout burns a tremendous amount of carbohydrates, some people say that you should eat 50 to 75 grams of carbs within 20 minutes of finishing your training, or your body may burn protein instead; that, in turn, can hinder muscle growth. Some everyday foods, such as carrot juice, are incredibly high in carbohydrates. Graham crackers and honey are also good. Eating these foods can be an excellent way to add quality carbs without taking a high-priced carb supplement.

FAT

Of all the macronutrients, fat has the worst reputation. People hear the word "fat" and think of obesity, but fat plays a vital role in a well-balanced diet.

It should account for 10% to 15% of your total caloric intake. Although fat is a secondary energy source, it contains twice as many calories per gram as protein or carbs. It's easy to see why people gain weight when they over eat fat. Fat cushions and protects the major organs and insulates the body from extreme cold, in addition to supplying energy. It also keeps our skin and hair healthy and distributes vitamins A, D, E, and K throughout our bodies. Saturated, unsaturated, and polyunsaturated fats are the three forms of fat. Saturated fat is primarily found in animal products such as cattle, lamb, pork, butter, and most cheeses. High cholesterol levels and an increased risk of heart disease have been linked to saturated fat. Foods heavy in saturated fat often taste wonderful, but you should limit your intake of this type of fat. Avocados, cashews, peanuts, peanut butter, olives, and olive oil are all abundant in unsaturated fat. This form of fat is recommended over saturated fat. Almonds, pecans, and walnuts contain polyunsaturated fat, like most margarine, mayonnaise, and soybean oil. According to medical research, some people who consume a lot of polyunsaturated fat and a little bit of saturated fat have lower cholesterol levels than others.

WATER

Water is also one of the fundamental nutrients, and many people neglect its significance. Water has numerous advantages. It is necessary for appropriate digestion, waste removal, and body temperature regulation. As an example of the necessity of water, people can go for weeks without food but only a few days without water. Muscles contain 72% water by weight. As a result, you lose muscle mass as you sweat during activity. During workouts, bring a water bottle with you and take periodic sips. Make an effort to drink before you become thirsty. Many experts say that everyone should drink eight 8-ounce glasses of water daily, and bodybuilders need to drink even more. Other liquids, such as juice, soft drinks, and coffee, do not count toward your water intake. Some bodybuilders make the mistake of trying to purge water from their bodies before a contest by using diuretics. They think that excess water beneath the skin reduces muscle definition. However, diuretics can be extremely dangerous or even fatal. Don't deprive your body of water.

VITAMINS

"Take your vitamins." That's advice many of our moms gave us while growing up, and they were right. Vitamins are organic substances that contribute to many essential bodily functions. We all need specific vitamins in certain amounts for optimum health. However, most nutritional experts believe that no one—not even a bodybuilder—needs vitamins in massive quantities. Some people take huge doses of Vitamin C to prevent colds, but this is generally not considered beneficial, and the result is simply high-priced urine. Vitamins fall into two categories: water-soluble and fat-soluble. Water-soluble vitamins cannot be stored in the body, and excess amounts are eliminated in urine. Because you can't retain them, you must take water-soluble vitamins daily if you don't get enough of them in your food. Some essential water-soluble vitamins include B1 (thiamin), B2 (riboflavin), B3 (niacin), B12 (cyanocobalamin), biotin, and Vitamin C (ascorbic acid). Unlike water-soluble vitamins, fat-soluble vitamins can be stored. As a result, they can be taken less frequently. A, D, E, and K are essential fat-soluble vitamins. Many experts feel that food loses a significant amount of its vitamin content due to processing and adding preservatives. Unfortunately, much of the food we eat nowadays is highly processed, making getting enough vitamins through diet alone challenging. Bodybuilders, due to their strenuous workouts, must take a basic vitamin supplement that can give adequate protection against vitamin insufficiency. Unless otherwise directed by your doctor, follow the dose recommendations on the bottle.

MINERALS

Unlike vitamins, minerals are inorganic substances. They promote the growth, maintenance, and repair of tissue. Minerals also assist in muscle contraction and the functioning of the nervous system. Some common minerals are calcium, magnesium, and potassium. Like vitamins, minerals are needed in relatively small amounts. A well-balanced diet may provide all the minerals you need, but it's wise to take a mineral supplement to prevent deficiency.

CALORIE CONSUMPTION

How many calories should you eat every day? No single solution applies to everyone, but as a bodybuilder, you require more calories than a sedentary person to gain muscle. Your metabolic rate and the intensity and frequency of your workouts determine how many more calories you need. Some people have a considerably higher metabolism than others, which means they burn much more calories than others with the same activity level. We discussed the three primary body types earlier in the book:

Ectomorph (naturally thin individuals).

Endomorph (naturally heavy people).

Mesomorph (people with good natural physiques who gain muscle quickly).

Knowing your body type will help to determine how much you should eat. You may need to eat practically constantly to maintain muscle mass or struggle to lose weight. In general, the more calories you require, the harder you train. Bodybuilders do not train at the same intensity all year. It is physically and mentally impossible to do so. When a competition is far away, they reduce their workout level; when an event comes, they raise their workout intensity. They alter their diet and calorie intake for each level. You should learn to be flexible with your calorie intake. For example, if you aren't going to the gym frequently to exercise, you should reduce your food intake. When a person stops lifting weight, muscle does not automatically turn to fat, causing the person to become overweight. Former bodybuilders become overweight when they stop lifting weights and don't reduce their calorie intake.

Diet and nutrition are critical components to achieving your fitness goals, whatever they may be. A "diet" does not imply that you will follow the Atkins or Jenny Craig diets, among others. You are on a diet if you are eating food. Your diet is simply what you put into your body. You are a machine that obtains energy from the food you consume. A diet is to a person what gasoline is to a car. Many people appear to be embarrassed by the word "diet," almost as if it were a disgrace.

What is shameful - is doing nothing about your situation. If you are weighty right now and want to get healthy, it's disgraceful to do nothing about it. If you are overweight and are contented with it, good for you! The shame is not in being overweight but in not taking action when you don't want to be overweight. If your exercise objective is to gain muscle mass, there is a good possibility you will need to adjust your diet to consume more healthy calories. If your fitness goals are to reduce excess fat, you may not need to consume fewer calories; instead, you should quit eating garbage, start eating good meals and get moving. You must look at yourself as a machine. McDonald's five times a week is not good for you. It is critical to provide clean, healthful nutrients.

If your calorie intake matches your workout intensity, you shouldn't develop a weight problem. Before you begin a serious weight training regimen, record your body weight and body fat percentage. The easiest, least expensive way to measure your body fat percentage is with a skinfold caliper, which resembles pliers. You pinch your skin at specific places on your body and use the caliper to measure the thickness of the pinched skin. You may arrange a more accurate body fat test through a physician or trainer where you're submerged in water. Keep a daily log of what you eat, including the number of calories and the amount of protein, carbohydrates, and fat. This will establish a baseline if you need to change your eating habits later. Don't automatically increase or decrease your calorie intake at the beginning. Start your workout program, continue eating as you usually would, and then see if you gain or lose weight.

If you're losing weight (and don't want to), you can afford to take in more calories. On the other side, you may discover that you are not losing weight despite intensive workouts. Because muscle weighs more than fat, it is possible—even expected—to gain weight while losing fat. Body weight alone is not an accurate indicator of fitness. However, you may discover that you still need to reduce your calorie intake to achieve your ideal weight. There's no need to become obsessed with calorie intake, counting the calories in every cracker or slice of bread.

This can be counterproductive and lead to binge eating due to starvation. As you become more experienced in bodybuilding, you'll be able to feel when your body needs food and trust your appetite. Bodybuilders must learn to personalize their eating habits and calorie intake just as they fine-tune their workout regimens.

MEAL FREQUENCY AND SELECTION

Recently, bodybuilders and nutritional experts have stressed the importance of frequent, smaller meals. Our bodies must be fed more than three times a day, mainly if we're engaged in heavy-weight training. When we eat fewer portions at each meal, our bodies digest the food more efficiently, and we don't feel "full" and sleepy. As a general guideline, you should eat five to six times daily or every two to three hours. Following this strategy will never be hungry enough to overeat or eat junk food. Planning is the key to successful meal frequency—developing the discipline to decide what to eat a few days ahead so that meals align with training and fitness goals. Few of us can plan to eat five or six meals at home every day. Therefore the advice is to "Begin eating correctly when you begin your program." Diet is essential for weight loss. Remember, training and eating go hand in hand. I don't disagree with taking supplements or vitamins—as long as it's in moderation." The meals you prepare can be small enough to be eaten quickly. By eating a small meal every few hours, you'll maintain your energy level better than if you were eating two or three large meals daily. If you have to eat at restaurants, you can still maintain a healthy eating plan if you carefully read menus and check the ingredients of menu items. These days, restaurants are accustomed to diners who watch what they eat. Ask the server for more details if necessary. It's not out of order to ask that an item be specially prepared if it's not on the menu. Be smart when grocery shopping— read labels. Fortunately, most packaged foods have a detailed ingredient labels, so it's easy to find the number of calories per serving and the amount of protein, carbohydrates, and fat. Pay attention to what you put in your body. You'll see the difference.

GENERAL EATING GUIDELINES

Because of the almost infinite variety of food choices, it's challenging to provide sample menus that would suit everyone and meet each person's individual needs. Other books are devoted entirely to diet and food preparation for bodybuilders. Here we'll touch on some of the broad "dos" and "don'ts" of food selection and preparation.

● Pay attention to your meals ratio of carbohydrates, protein, and fat. Ideally, your diet should consist of about 50% carbs, 35% protein, and 15% fat.

● Choose fresh fruits and vegetables instead of canned or frozen ones. The latter often contain sugar, salt, and preservatives that can be harmful.

● Select fresh meats instead of processed meats (like lunch meat) for the same reason you choose fresh fruits and vegetables.

● Eat white meat (such as chicken breasts) instead of dark meat (such as chicken thighs) because white meat has less fat. Remove the skin to reduce the fat further

● Eat fish, which typically has even less fat than white meat. A popular choice for bodybuilders is tuna, inexpensive and easy to take since it's canned and requires no refrigeration. Select tuna that's packed in spring water, not oil. The oil contains many useless calories.

● Broil or bake your meat, poultry, or fish. Never fry it.

● Don't overcook vegetables because overcooking destroys many of the vitamins and minerals they contain.

● Buy low-fat or no-fat versions of dairy products like milk and yogurt.

- Use fewer egg yolks because they're high in fat and cholesterol. You don't have to give them up entirely; if you fix three scrambled eggs, you can include one yolk and toss the other two.

- Choose whole grain bread, which has more fiber and is more nutritious than bread made with white, processed flour.

- Avoid toppings that are high in calories and fat. A dry baked potato is excellent, but a baked potato with butter and sour cream is not. Lettuce has almost no calories or fat until you add salad dressing, so be sure to pick a dressing that's low-fat or no-fat. When eating meats, avoid gravy. With pasta, stay away from sauces made with heavy cream.

- Pick fruit instead of candy if you want to eat sweets. Go easy on fruits and fruit juices, however, because even though they're healthier than candy and soft drinks, they're still rich in sugar and calories.

- Learn to discipline yourself, so you don't succumb to impulsive eating. We all "fall off the wagon" sometimes and eat foods that aren't a part of our recommended diet. Just try to ensure that you do so occasionally, and then resume your eating plan.

- Avoid fad diets that recommend drastically cutting back or eliminating major nutrients, such as carbohydrates.

- Don't try to shed more than 2 pounds a week if you want to lose weight.

- Add variety to your diet. Eat a wide range of healthy foods. The more you enjoy your food, the more likely you will stick with good eating habits.

- Make wise use of excellent meal replacement products, such as powders and drinks. If you're short on time, you can take them instead of preparing a meal. However, never rely entirely on replacement products and supplements; they can't take the place of healthy eating.

- Eat nuts and dried fruit for a quick snack, but in moderation.

- Always eat breakfast. Some people skip breakfast to cut calories, but that's not wise. You need a good supply of fuel to start your day. Otherwise, you may be low on energy and tempted to eat junk food.

- Wait one hour after eating to work out so you can properly digest your food.

SUPPLEMENTS TO CONSIDER

Many calisthenics athletes do not take supplements, but they are something you might like to consider. Here are the top 5 for you to think about. Although supplements cannot replace proper nutrition, they can help you hit your fitness goals faster. The appropriate supplements can help improve your health, performance, and physique regardless of your training goals.

Protein
Protein supplements work quickly and affordably, allowing you to fulfill your daily protein goals even when you're on the go. Because whey protein digests quickly and easily, it is an excellent post-workout protein source.

Fish Oil
The multiple benefits of fish oil are due to its high quantities of omega-3 fatty acids. Omega-3 fatty acids are classified as necessary fatty acids. This suggests that they are required for human health yet are not produced by the body. Fish oil is a crucial supplement for anyone looking to build muscle, burn fat, or improve their overall health.

Branched Chain Amino Acids
When consumed during training, BCAAs can advance prolonged performance and promote recovery. BCAAs may also reduce muscle breakdown (catabolism), potentially leading to total muscle growth.

Glutamine
Glutamine is a protein adaptogenic amino acid. It is the most abundant amino acid in skeletal muscle and is crucial to immune system health and overall bodily wellness. Glutamate supplements can provide additional benefits to help grow muscle mass.

Creatine

Creatine is one of the most thoroughly researched supplements on the market. It has been shown to improve sprint times and the performance of athletes who participate in high-intensity activities like weightlifting and strength training.

STARTING A WORKOUT

When you begin weightlifting, you need to address two fundamental questions:
1. Where should I train?
2. Should I train alone or with a partner? Today, good gyms are nearly everywhere.

Finding a place to train is not nearly as difficult as it used to be. In shopping for a gym, however, location is critical. If you have to drive 45 minutes to get there, you probably won't go very often—and your progress will suffer. On the other hand, if the gym is just around the corner, you're much more likely to work out regularly. Gyms, like people, have personalities. Some attract those who are interested in overall fitness. People who go to these gyms might want to take aerobics classes, do yoga, swim, or jog— but not necessarily lift the weight. You can undoubtedly pursue bodybuilding in a gym like this, as long as it has free weights and machines available. However, if you're the only bodybuilder in the gym, you may feel uncomfortable over time. As a result, your intensity—and the frequency of your workouts—may wane. If you intend to be a serious bodybuilder, you're probably better off joining a gym geared toward "iron heads," fellow hard-core lifters. These folks typically don't care about fancy dressing areas, saunas, or aerobics classes.

They're only interested in rows and rows of barbells and machines. Does that describe you? If you're an iron head, you'll thrive in an environment like this. You'll be more likely to train with intensity because others are training hard, too. Nowadays, some people train at home instead of joining a gym. It's now possible to buy first-class, gym-quality workout equipment for your home because it has come down enough in both price and size that it's practical to keep in a spare bedroom. However, before you shell out thousands of dollars for equipment, buy an inexpensive barbell set, which can cost $50 to $100. A basic barbell set will allow you to learn the proper lifting form, get used to handling weights, and find out if you enjoy weight training and like working out at home.

If so, you can steadily add to and upgrade your equipment.

Virtually all serious bodybuilders, however, eventually train at a gym. The reasons are apparent. Good gyms have a far more extensive assortment of weights and machines than you could probably afford to buy for your home. At a gym, you also have plenty of people to "spot" you—lend a hand if you've grabbed too much weight. This leads to the question of a training partner. Do you need one? There's no answer that's right for everyone. Perhaps you thrive on the rapport that develops between regular training buddies. If you know someone is waiting for you at the gym, you may be more likely to show up and train harder. In addition, some exercises are challenging (and may even be dangerous) to perform alone. Still, there are valid reasons not to have a training partner. Perhaps you're self-motivated and don't need anyone else to fuel your intensity. Working with a partner might slow your workouts and impede your progress. Bodybuilding, after all, is fundamentally an individual sport. Give it some thought. You probably already know whether you'd benefit from a training partner—or not. Another critical element in bodybuilding is diet. We'll devote an entire chapter to nutrition and diet later, but remember that what you eat considerably affects your muscle development. If you're undisciplined in your eating—and if you have no desire to change—you severely limit your chances for success. You don't have to become a food fanatic or take expensive, exotic supplements, but you must pay attention to your food intake. Without an awareness of what you eat and when and how much you eat, you won't be able to make the dietary adjustments necessary for peak muscle development.

Many bodybuilders swear by dietary supplements, but the best supplements in the world can't take the place of intense, regular training. There's no such thing as a magic elixir or a "workout in a jar," so beware of products that promise unbelievable results. The saying goes, "If it sounds too good to be true, it probably is." Besides being ineffective, supplements may contain unproven and even dangerous ingredients.

For advanced bodybuilders with thorough nutrition knowledge, supplements can be helpful and provide an extra edge in competition. Just don't begin bodybuilding with the idea that a pill or a powder can take the place of dedication and sweat. There are no shortcuts. Finally, before you start serious weight training, get a thorough physical exam. Even young people can have potentially serious health problems that are undiagnosed. A checkup is usually quick, easy, and inexpensive. When it's over, you'll have the peace of mind to let you train your hardest.

First Routines

All top bodybuilders learn to tailor their workouts to what's effective for them and what helps them achieve their goals. Because no two people are alike, exercises that work great for one bodybuilder may produce poor results for another. As you gain experience, you'll learn which exercises are best for you and how to structure your workouts. Still, when starting, everyone should become familiar with some well-established, basic weightlifting exercises. These cover all the major muscle groups: shoulder, chest, arm, leg, and abdomen. Once you become comfortable with these—and notice how your muscles respond—you'll be in a position to customize your routines.

These 19 basic exercises provide the foundation on which you can develop your bodybuilder's physique. Tried and-true exercises such as Bench Press, Curls, and Squats are so effective that even champion bodybuilders never abandon them entirely. Top competitors constantly tinker with their regimen, trying different exercises that they hope will take them to the next level. Still, they never stray far from the core exercises they mastered as beginners.

Take a lesson from the pros. Learn these basic exercises by heart. And keep this in mind: Look for steady, consistent progress, not overnight miracles. Many budding bodybuilders, unfortunately, have unrealistic expectations and underestimate the time it will take to reshape their physiques. Sadly, many become discouraged and give up bodybuilding before discovering their potential. The prize in bodybuilding—as in most endeavors— usually goes to the turtle, not the hare. With that said, let's recap some of the appeals of bodybuilding to energize you as you begin. While none of us can control our genes—nature has predetermined our height and body shape to a large extent—each of us can improve the body we were born with, and there's no better way to do this than weight lifting.

Most bodybuilders choose the sport because they feel they are too skinny or fat or may think they have a mediocre build. Weight lifting lets you sculpt and reshape your body. By choosing the right exercises and performing them properly, you can add muscle here, lose fat there, and tone up from head to toe.

STRETCHING AND WARMING UP

Athletes from all sports understand the value of stretching and preparing their bodies for a strenuous workout. You are far more likely to strain a muscle, ligament, or tendon if you do not stretch. Even a minor injury can keep you out of the gym for several days or weeks, slowing your progress significantly. Even when done correctly, weight training puts a lot of strain on your body. While the stress of weight resistance causes muscle growth, lifting heavy weights can harm your body if not properly prepared. This is where stretching and warming up come in.

They are two separate steps, though they are frequently combined. Warming up entails movement. Light aerobic activity, such as riding a stationary bike or walking on a treadmill, is the best example. The goal is to increase your heart rate, improve your breathing, and pump your blood faster. Your body is literally "warming up" for a complete workout. Stretching, on the other hand, is a static exercise in which you stand or sit still while slowly extending your muscles to make them more limber. The more you stretch your muscles, the bigger they will grow. Most experts recommend warming up before stretching. Why? You're far more likely to pull a muscle if you stretch when your body is cold. A good warm-up should take about 10 minutes—long enough to work up a light sweat but not so long that you become fatigued and have less energy for your upcoming weight training.

It's time to stretch after you've warmed up. Stretching is done to increase flexibility and prevent injuries while lifting. If you're in a hurry and want to start lifting immediately, skipping stretching is a bad idea. "I stretch a lot," top bodybuilder Mike Matarazzo says. "You have to stay loose. Find a way to stretch whatever muscles you're working." To avoid injury and maximize benefits, we must adequately prepare our bodies for demanding workouts, especially as we get older.

Don't shortchange yourself. Stretching has other benefits besides cutting down on injuries. It helps to relieve tension and focuses your mind on your approaching workout. Stretching also lengthens your muscles and gives you a leaner, more toned appearance—a massive asset for competition. "Many people don't realize the value of stretching to strengthen and elongate the muscle and help it grow," said Lee Labrada, two-time Mr. Olympia runner-up. Stretching, however, must be done properly. It should always be gradual and gentle, with no bouncing or jerking movements. It may take up to 30 seconds to reach the fully stretched position; if you rush it, you won't get the full benefit. Stretching is an excellent pre-workout activity, but many bodybuilders also stretch during and after workouts.

Muscles can become tense and tight during intense lifting, and stretching during a workout can help make them limber and ready to lift some more. After a workout, stretching is an excellent way to cool down. For one thing, it's much easier on your body to bring your heart and breathing rates down gradually than to stop exercising suddenly. In addition, stretching after a workout helps prevent muscle soreness and promotes faster muscle recovery. After a workout, as your muscles recover, most muscle growth occurs.

Names of Muscles

Upper Body

- Pectorals ("pecs"—chest muscles)
- Deltoids ("delts"—rounded muscles at the top of the shoulders)
- Latissimus Dorsi muscles ("lats"— muscles extending from under the armpits across the back to the spine)
- Trapezius muscles ("traps"—muscles extending from the neck to the middle of the back)
- Spinal erectors (horizontal muscles extending down the back to just above the waist)
- Oblique's (muscles on the side of the torso, next to the abdominals)
- Intercostals (diagonal muscles across the ribs, just above the abdominals)
- Serratus muscles (diagonal muscles slightly above the intercostal, near the pectorals)
- Abdominals ("abs"—vertical muscles extending the length of the abdomen)

Arms

- Biceps
- Triceps
- Forearm flexors (muscles of the inside of the forearm)
- Forearm extensors (muscles of the outside of the forearm)

Legs

- Quadriceps ("quads"—muscles at the front of the thigh)
- Hamstrings (muscles that extend from the back of the thigh to the lower leg)
- Gastrocnemius muscles (upper calf muscles)
- Soleus muscles (lower calf muscles)
- Buttocks
- Gluteus Maximus muscles ("glutes"— muscles of the buttocks)

STRETCHING EXERCISES

The following basic stretching exercises cover all the major muscle groups.

Standing Torso Bend

The area worked: Oblique's
Instructions:

Place your feet slightly wider than shoulder-width apart and your arms at your sides. Raise your right arm overhead, elbow bent. Keep your arm there and lean as far to the left as you can while keeping your feet stable. Slide your left arm down the outside of your left leg to lean further. Hold for about 15 seconds before returning to the starting position. Lean to the right and repeat with your left arm overhead. You can also perform the exercise while raising both arms overhead at the same time.

Forward Bend

Areas worked: Lower back, hamstrings

Instructions: Stand upright, with your feet together. Bend forward gradually and grab the backs of your calves. Slowly try to reach down farther. See if you can touch the backs of your ankles, but don't strain. Lower your head toward your shins to let you reach farther down. When you're at the lowest point you can comfortably maintain, hold the position for 30 seconds.

Seated Torso Bend

Areas worked: Oblique's, lower back, spine

Instructions: Sit on the floor, your legs outstretched in front of you. Keep your left leg on the floor and bend your right leg up so your knee is chest high. Twist your torso as far to the right as you can while keeping your buttocks on the floor. Support yourself by extending your right arm behind you. Place your left elbow on the outside of your right knee to aid in twisting. Hold the position for 30 seconds after you've twisted as far as you can. Then, with your left leg bent at the knee and twisting to the left, repeat.

V-Stretch

Areas worked: Hamstrings lower back

Instructions: Sit on the floor with your knees locked and legs extended in a wide V. Bend forward and extend your arms in front of you as far as possible. With your fingers touching the floor, hold the position for 10 seconds. Then gradually turn to your right and grab your right ankle. Hold for 10 seconds. Return to the starting position. Then turn and grab your left ankle, holding for 10 seconds.

Lunges

Areas worked: Inner thighs, glutes

Instructions: Crouch on the floor, your left leg extended behind you, and your right leg bent so your thigh is parallel to the floor. Lean forward until your torso is in contact with your right thigh. Place your fingers on the floor directly below your shoulders. Keep your head up and your gaze fixed ahead. Stretch your torso forward and down for 15 seconds. Return to your starting position by standing. Rep with your right leg in front of you and your left leg bent.

Groin Stretch

Areas worked: Groin muscles, inner thighs

Instructions: Sit on the floor with your knees bent and turned outward. Pull your feet as close to your buttocks as possible. Grab the outer front edges of your feet, and rest your elbows on your thighs. Slowly press down on your legs, lowering them closer to the floor. (Don't press too far. Your knees should stop about a foot from the floor.) At the lowest point, hold for 15 seconds.

Leg Crossover

Areas worked: Lower back, hips, and thighs

Instructions: Lie on your back with your legs together and straight. Extend your arms to the side at a 90-degree angle to your torso. While keeping your arms stationary, lift your right leg straight up, then cross it over your left leg. Touch your right toes to the floor, even with your knee. (It is important to keep your arms and left leg stationary for maximum benefit.) Hold for 15 seconds. Repeat, lifting your left leg and crossing it over your right leg.

Back Roll

Area worked: Mid-back

Instructions: Lie on your back with your knees drawn up to your chest. Grab the tops of your shins and press your legs toward your chest. Hold the position for 15 seconds. Then, slowly rock backward until your weight is supported by your shoulder blades. Maintain your equilibrium. Maintain your grip on your legs. (Caution: If this makes you feel uncomfortable, don't do it. Roll forward until your weight is back on your back.) Hold the position for 15 seconds.

Calf Stretch

Area worked: Calves

Instructions: Stand about an arm's length from a wall. Lean forward and place both palms on the wall. Keep your legs straight and together. Slowly lean your head forward until it touches the wall. Keep your feet flat on the floor and feel your calf muscles stretch. Hold for 15 seconds. Then rise up on your toes to stretch farther. Hold for another 15 seconds.

Triceps Stretch

Area worked: Triceps

Instructions: Position your feet shoulder-width apart. Raise and bend your left arm at the elbow. Place your left hand on your right shoulder blade, behind your head. Your left forearm should be pressed on your skull. Gently press down on your left elbow with your right hand. Your left hand should slide slightly downward. Hold for 15 seconds at the lowest point you can comfortably maintain. Rep with your right arm behind your head and your left hand pressing down.

Crunches

Area worked: Abs

Instructions: Lie on your back on the floor in front of a flat bench. Bend your knees and place the backs of your calves on top of the bench. Clasp your hands behind your head. Exhale and raise your head and shoulders toward your knees, keeping your back on the floor. Inhale and lower yourself to the floor. Repeat. (This is a very short movement. It's not a full sit-up, in which you touch your elbows to your knees. It's critical to do it slowly and deliberately in order to get the full effect.)

Neck Roll

Area worked: Neck

Instructions: Stand with your feet about shoulder-width apart. Place your palms on either side of your waist or let your arms hang straight down. Bend your head forward until your chin almost touches your chest. Hold for 15 seconds. Then slowly rotate your head to the right, making a complete circle around your body. Do this 3 times, slowly. Then reverse and rotate your head to the left, making a circle 3 times.

96

LIFTING BASICS

Before getting into the basic weightlifting routines, we must discuss specific training difficulties. These include the proper amount of repetitions and sets, proper breathing, the length and frequency of your workouts, warm-up sets, and how to deal with soreness.

Repetitions

Regardless of the exercise, choose a weight that permits you to complete 8 to 10 repetitions or reps comfortably. Work your way up to 12 to 15 reps as you gain strength. Then, add more weight (5 or 10 pounds) and reduce the number of reps to 8 to 10. Work your way up to 12 to 15 reps with the heavier weight. As weight training develops, follow this cycle: increase reps, then add weight. Work out with around 75% of the weight you can lift once. For instance, if you can bench press 100 pounds once, you should work out with about 75 pounds and do 8 to 10 reps. However, there's no need to repeatedly find out how much weight you can lift at one time. After all, you're not training to be a powerlifter, where lifting the maximum weight is the goal. You're interested in being a bodybuilder, where muscle development is the objective. This is achieved by doing multiple reps in a smooth, rhythmic manner with a weight you can handle.

Sets

Some folks get sets and repetitions mixed up. The number of repetitions refers to how many times you lift a weight. The number of sets refers to how many times you do an exercise. For example, ten reps of Bench Press equals one set. If you add ten additional reps, that's two sets—and so on. As a novice, you should begin with two sets for every exercise, though one set is sufficient until you are comfortable lifting.

97

Although experienced bodybuilders may perform ten or more sets of an exercise, some experts argue that doing so is harmful. You can do additional sets as you gain experience. Limit yourself to two, resting about one minute between sets. The number of sets you do is less important than your lifting intensity. "More [sets] aren't better," says Paul DeMayo, a top bodybuilder. "It's what you do in the amount of time. I don't hang around. People are amazed that I progress because they're convinced you have to be in there four, five, six hours a day."

Breathing

Many starting weight lifters do not breathe correctly. It's normal to hold your breath when doing a workout, but this might be dangerous. You may become so dizzy and weak that you pass out. Instead, inhale and exhale slowly and steadily. Inhale at the easiest section of a workout (while reducing the weight) and exhale during the more difficult part (lifting). You should coordinate your breathing with your lifting. Proper breathing will quickly become second nature, and you will no longer have to worry about it.

Workout Duration and Frequency

There are two main ways to schedule your workouts. You can train all your muscles three times a week—such as on Monday, Wednesday, and Friday— or you can train only some of your muscles at a time and work out six days a week. You have an option. Just make sure you're not training seven days a week. At least one day is required for your muscles to recuperate and grow. Some people enjoy the sense of working all of their muscles at once, then resting for a day before doing another full-body workout. Others focus on specific muscles one day, such as the shoulders, chest, and back, and then switch to other muscles the next. If you opt to train six days a week, keep your workouts brief.

If you lift for an extended period, your form may deteriorate. If you're a beginner, you can complete a terrific workout in 45 minutes if you focus. That allows enough exercise time to cover all the major muscle groups. Once you become more experienced, you can extend your workouts by increasing the number of sets and exercises. The length of your workouts may vary, depending on whether you use free weights— barbells and dumbbells—or machines. It usually takes longer to lift with free weights because you have to add and remove weight plates between exercises. You place a pin in the weight stack with machines and start lifting. Many elite bodybuilders train nearly entirely with free weights, believing that barbells and dumbbells provide more variation in their routines. Machines, for example, often limit the lifting action; that is, the weights go only along a specific path. To reach your aims, you can infinitely change the lifting motion with free weights. Machines, on the other hand, have advantages. On machines, you can do some highly effective exercises that are tough to do with free weights. Furthermore, machines are frequently safer than barbells because you do not have to support the entire weight. Regardless of how you plan your workout or whether you use free weights or machines, it's important to determine what time of day is best for you to train and establish a routine.

Some people have more energy in the morning and like to work out then. Others are more alert later in the day or at night. It's not the time of day that matters; the intensity matters. If you can work out harder at 7 A.M., that's the time to do it. If you can train harder at 7 P.M., that's the time to do it. Either way, establish a routine. Don't work out at 6 A.M. one day, at 10 P.M. the next, and noon the following day. Your body needs a regular schedule. As you work out, keep in mind that improvement in bodybuilding rarely occurs in a straight line. Instead, you'll most likely make progress in bursts. You could go weeks or even months without noticing any improvement. However, if you continue to train, the benefits will return. Simply be consistent and avoid making excuses to skip workouts. "Unless you are so ill that you must stay in bed," says former Mr. Universe Boyer Coe, "you should never miss a scheduled workout." "One missed workout can set your progress back by up to a week because missing a training session has negative consequences."

Warm-Up Sets

We talked about warming up before a workout before. 5 to 10 minutes of light cardiovascular activity, such as riding a stationary bike or utilizing a stair machine, is ideal. This gets your body ready for lifting. Warm-up sets are another type of warm-up that is equally important. This entails practicing lightweight sets before performing the same exercise with your regular training weight. You should do warm-up sets with half the weight and twice the reps. Warm up by doing 15 reps of Bench Press with 75 pounds if you usually do eight reps with 150 pounds. With the lighter weight and higher reps, you can concentrate on proper lifting form and prepare your muscles for the heavier weight. As you become more advanced, warm-up sets are even more critical. Some competitive bodybuilders who use extremely heavy weights do several warm-up sets for each exercise. This helps them avoid injury.

Soreness vs. Pain

Muscle discomfort is a normal aspect of the bodybuilding process. In reality, mild soreness indicates that you're performing workouts correctly and making improvements. A challenging workout that leaves your muscles pumped and sore has an amazing, fulfilling feeling to it. The pain will subside in a day or two and will not interfere with your next workout. However, discomfort is not a good indicator; therefore, learning to distinguish between soreness and pain is critical. For example, if your back suffers so severely that you can scarcely stand, the cause is improper lifting. Pain is a warning sign that you might be causing an injury that could sideline you for weeks. If you feel a sharp, sudden pain during lifting, stop immediately. By doing so, you're not being a wimp—you're being smart. If the pain persists, seek medical attention. "No pain, no gain" is a popular term in sports. We might amend it for bodybuilding to "No soreness, no gain."

BASIC EXERCISES

Upper Body

Bench Press

Primary muscles used: Chest

Technique: Lie down on a flat bench with uprights for holding a barbell. Place your feet at the end of the bench on the floor. Grab the bar above your head using an overhand grip (palms down, thumbs in) and slightly wider than shoulder-width apart. Lift the bar straight up from the supports, keeping your elbows locked. As you rise, exhale. Inhale, then slowly lower the bar until it rests on the highest point of your chest. Allow the bar to rest for a second before exhaling and pushing the bar straight up, locking your elbows again. Repeat.

Dumbbell Fly

Primary muscles used: Chest

Technique: Lie on a flat bench with no supports for a barbell. Grab a dumbbell in each hand, with your arms extended and even with the top of the bench. Bend your elbows slightly. Then raise the dumbbells in front of you, in line with your chest, until they touch. Make sure you have a secure grip, then exhale and lower the dumbbells to your sides (along the same path) until they are even with the top of the bench. Hold for a second, then exhale and lift the dumbbells again until they touch. Repeat.

NOTE: This exercise can also be done on a common machine, often called a "pec deck." Sit on a bench and bend your arms at the elbow in front of you, with your forearms in a vertical position. Place your forearms against pads in front of your shoulders. Exhale and press against the pads together until they touch in front of your chest. Hold, then inhale and let the pads return to the starting position. Repeat.

Dips

Primary muscles used: Chest

Technique: This workout does not require the use of weights; instead, your body weight provides all of the resistance. Locate a pair of "dip bars," which are free-standing, parallel bars that are slightly broader than your shoulders and about chest high. Place your palms on top of the bars while standing between the bars. Jump up slowly and straighten your arms until your elbows lock. Your feet should be about a foot above the ground, and your waist should be a few inches above the bars. Inhale and gently lower yourself until your chest is parallel to the bars. To keep your feet from contacting the floor, bend your knees. Exhale after a second and push yourself back up until your elbows lock. Repeat.

Upright Row

Primary muscles used: Lats (back)

Technique: Stand with your feet slightly more than shoulder-width apart. Grab a barbell off the floor with an overhand grip (palms down, thumbs in) and your hands 8 to 10 inches apart. Let the bar rest against your thighs. Exhale and lift the bar straight up, keeping it close to your body, until it almost touches your chin. Keep your back straight and your legs straight as you lift. Hold the barbell under your chin for a second, then inhale and lower it to the starting position in front of your thighs. Repeat.

Lat Pulldown

Primary muscles used: Lats (back)

Technique: This exercise is done on a machine that's found in almost every gym. It has a long horizontal bar overhead that's attached to a stack of weights by a cable. Kneel on the floor under the bar (or sit on a bench, if one is available). Extend your arms overhead and grab the bar with an overhand grip and your hands 2 to 3 inches from the ends. Exhale as you pull the bar down smoothly in front of your face until it touches your chest. Hold for a second, then inhale and gradually let the bar return to the starting position. Repeat.

Lateral Raise

Primary muscles used: Shoulders

Technique: Stand and hold a dumbbell on each side of your body. Lean forward at the waist slightly, and bend your elbows a little. Exhale and slowly raise your arms, keeping them in line with your shoulders. Stop when the dumbbells are slightly higher than your shoulders. Don't let your body rock—this reduces the benefit to your shoulders. Hold the dumbbells at the topmost point for a second, then inhale and slowly lower them to your side. Repeat.

Military Press

Primary muscles used: Shoulders

Technique: This exercise can be performed with either a barbell or a machine. If you utilize a barbell, you should: Take an overhand hold on a barbell and set your hands slightly wider than shoulder-width apart. Hold the barbell against your thighs. Then, raise the barbell until it rests on top of your chest. (For support, place your palms behind the bar.) Lift the barbell above your head until your elbows lock. Keep your legs still. Hold for a second, then slowly drop the barbell until it rests again against your chest. Start the next rep from your chest. If you use a machine: Sit on a bench and grab the handle that's about even with your shoulders and connected.

Arms

Curls

Primary muscles used: Biceps

Technique: Grab a barbell with an underhand grip (palms up, thumbs out) and your hands about shoulder-width apart. Stand and let the barbell rest against your thighs. Keeping your elbows close to your sides, exhale and raise the bar to your chest. Hold for a moment, then inhale and lower the bar to your thighs. Keep your elbows and upper arms stationary. Repeat.

Preacher Curl

Primary muscles used: Biceps

Technique: This exercise uses a "preacher bench," which has a small seat and an armrest platform about chest high that slopes down and away from the seat. Sit on the seat and place the backs of your upper arms on the sloping platform. Stretch your arms and grab a barbell with an underhand grip. Exhale and bend your arms, slowly bringing the barbell to the top of the platform (near your chin). Pause, then inhale and lower the barbell to the bottom of the platform, locking your elbows. Repeat. NOTE: By not permitting use of your legs or upper body, this exercise isolates your biceps more than standing Curls.

Triceps Pushdown

Primary muscles used: Triceps

Technique: This exercise is similar to the last Lat Pulldown. Place yourself in front of the machine, which has a long horizontal bar above it. With your hands 8 to 10 inches apart, grab the bar with an overhand hold. Lower the bar till it is parallel to your chest. Tuck your elbows in close to your sides. Now exhale and press down on the bar using only your upper arms. When the bar reaches your thighs, come to a complete stop. Hold, then inhale and slowly raise the bar to the beginning position in front of your chest. Keep your upper arms parallel to the ground. Repeat.

 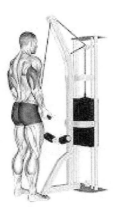

Dips Behind The Back

Primary muscles used:

Triceps Technique: This exercise is identical to the last exercise, parallel bar dips. There are no weights used. Place two normal flat benches 4 to 5 feet apart, parallel to each other. Position your heels on one bench and your palms on the other. Your buttocks will be dangling in midair, directly in front of the back bench. Your body will form a L shape, with your legs parallel to the floor and your torso at a 90-degree angle. Inhale, bend your elbows, and slowly drop your buttocks until they almost touch the floor. Keep your heels on the front bench. Hold your body as low as possible for a second, then exhale and raise your body to the starting position, locking your elbows. Repeat.

Dumbbell Wrist Curl

Primary muscles used: Forearms

Technique: Sit on a standard flat bench. Using an underhand grip, grab a dumbbell in one hand. Lean forward and rest your forearm on your thigh, your wrist just above your knee. Allow the dumbbell to roll toward the tips of your fingers as you lower your wrist toward the floor. Then, return your wrist to your body, allowing the dumbbell to roll onto your palm. Repeat. Stretch your forearm muscles. Repeat with your opposing arm.

Legs

Leg Extension

Primary muscles used: Thighs

Technique: This exercise uses a machine with a flat bench and two cylinder-shaped pads attached to a weight stack. Sit on the end of the bench with your legs hanging straight down from your knees. Place your shins against the backs of the pads. Grab the sides of the bench (or handles if it has them) and lift your legs straight up, raising the weight stack. Stop when your knees lock. Hold, then inhale and lower the pads to the starting position. Repeat.

Squats

Primary muscles used: Thighs

Technique: Begin with a barbell at shoulder height lying on a rack. Stand with your back to the bar, slightly bend your knees, and allow the bar to touch the back of your shoulders. Take an overhand grip with your hands somewhat wider than shoulder width apart. Lift the bar carefully from the rack. Check that you have a firm grasp and a stable footing. Inhale and bend your knees until your thighs are parallel to the floor, then place the bar against the back of your shoulders. Hold for a moment, then exhale and slowly rise, straightening your legs until you reach your starting position. Repeat.

NOTE: This exercise can be dangerous if done improperly. As you lower yourself, keep the bar directly above your ankles; don't let the weight get too far in front of or behind your body, or you may lose your balance. Also, keep your head up and your eyes looking forward. This ensures that your thighs, not your back, bear most of the weight.

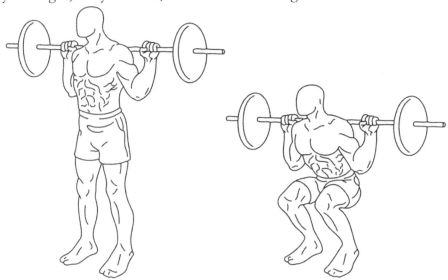

Leg Curl

Primary muscles used: Hamstrings

Technique: This exercise is done on a machine with a flat or inverted-V bench. Lie face down on the bench, and place your ankles under two cylinder-shaped pads. Bend your knees, then exhale and lift your lower legs until your feet almost touch your buttocks. Hold, then inhale and let the weights return your ankles to the starting position. Repeat.

Calf Raise

Primary muscles used: Calves

Technique: This exercise begins similarly to the Squats described above. Place your back to a barbell resting on a shoulder-height rack. Take an overhand grip on the bar, with your hands somewhat wider than shoulder width apart. Remove the bar from the rack and position it carefully on top of your shoulders. Place the balls of your feet on a 2 inch-high block, with your heels extended over the edge of the block. Exhale and raise your heels as high as you can while still holding the barbell solidly on your shoulders. Hold, then inhale and lower your heels to the floor. Repeat.

Abs

Crunches

Primary muscles used: Abs

Technique: Lie on your back on the floor in front of a flat bench. Bend your knees and place the backs of your calves on top of the bench. Clasp your hands behind your head. Exhale and raise your head and shoulders toward your knees, keeping your back on the floor. Inhale and lower yourself to the floor. Repeat. NOTE: This is a very short movement. It's critical to do it slowly and deliberately to get the full effect.

Leg Lifts

Primary muscles used: Abs

Technique: Lie on your back on a flat bench, buttocks at one end, legs hanging loosely. Straighten your legs until they are parallel to the floor and even with the bench's top. Grab the bench's sides for support. Exhale and raise your legs overhead until they are perpendicular to the floor, keeping your legs together and straight. Pause for a moment, then slowly lower them back to their initial position. Repeat.

GETTING FAMILIAR WITH BASIC GYM EQUIPMENT

Free weights: barbells and dumbbells, the most basic weightlifting equipment. A barbell is a straight bar about 60 inches long. Dumbbells are much shorter, about 14 inches long. Weights are placed on the ends of both types of bars for resistance.

Plates: thin, circular weights that go on barbells and dumbbells. The lightest plates usually weigh 2.5 pounds, and plates increase in weight incrementally—5 pounds, 10 pounds, etc.—up to about 50 pounds each. You place a combination of different-sized plates on barbells and dumbbells to create the weight you want for an exercise.

Collars: are metal devices of varying styles that are fastened on the ends of barbells and dumbbells to keep the plates in place.

Machines: are the other equipment (besides barbells and dumbbells) used in weight lifting. Machines differ in size, shape, and complexity, using a combination of weights, pulleys, and cables. Typically, you sit on a bench, grab a handle, and push or pull a stack of weights. You select the amount of weight you want by inserting a metal pin in a specific position in the weight stack.

Bench: a fundamental piece of equipment used for many lifting exercises. Flat benches, for instance, are used in one of the most common chest exercises, Bench Press. Some exercises call for incline benches, where the top of the bench is higher than the bottom. There are also decline benches, where the base is higher than the top. Finally, a special bench called a preacher bench is designed for Curls, a common biceps exercise.

Gloves: gloves, usually leather, help you grip the bar better. They can also help reduce calluses, which are common among weight lifters. Often the palms of gloves are padded slightly to make lifting more comfortable. The fingers of a glove usually stop at the middle knuckle, allowing you to get your fingertips on the barbell, dumbbell, or machine for greater sensitivity and control.

Weightlifting belt: a wide, heavy belt often made of leather or reinforced nylon. It helps stabilize your back and prevent injuries during heavy lifting. Some bodybuilders wear a belt while performing all their exercises. Others prefer to use a belt only when lifting maximum weight.

Wraps: cloth or elastic bands that you place around your elbows or knees during heavy lifting. Wraps support the joints and help you avoid injury.

Logbook: a journal used to record workout regimen and progress. You write down which exercises you performed, the weight, the number of repetitions, etc. Logs can be very useful in planning workouts. Tape measure, scale, and camera: tools used to document your weight and the size of your muscles before you begin bodybuilding so that you have a baseline by which to gauge your progress. Body weight can be deceiving because muscle weighs more than fat. It's possible to increase your weight at the same time that you're losing fat. Still, it's essential to know your body weight as you begin. After weighing yourself, take measurements of your chest, shoulders, biceps, waist, thighs, and calves. Finally, get someone to take photos of you wearing shorts in several relaxed and flexed poses. As you make progress, you can compare yourself to the photos.

TRAINING TERMS

Burn: the slightly painful but exhilarating sensation you get in a muscle at the end of a strenuous exercise. Muscle failure: a condition in which your muscles become so exhausted that you can't perform another repetition.

Pump: the dramatic muscle expansion after an intense exercise before the muscles return to their normal size. Rep: short for "repetitions." The number of reps is the number of times you complete an exercise movement.

Ripped: a term to describe extreme muscle definition. Bodybuilders try to become "ripped"—developing muscles that stand out from others. Another term for ripped is "cut."

Routine: the sequence of exercises that make up a workout. Your training, or regimen, will vary over time as you progress and concentrate on different muscles. Set: a group of repetitions. For instance, if you do eight reps of an exercise, that's one set. If you follow it up with another eight reps, that's two sets of eight reps.

Spotter: a person who stands beside you during an exercise to assist if necessary. A spotter can help you perform a final rep after your muscles become fatigued. Or a spotter can take a barbell from you if you've tried to lift too much.

Training partner: a person you work out with regularly. Many bodybuilders have regular training partners. They find that partners help motivate them to achieve greater intensity during workouts. Partners can also serve as spotters.

Vascularity: the prominence of veins on a bodybuilder's well-developed physique. As a person becomes more "ripped," veins in the arms, chest, legs and other areas begin to stand out.

Intermediate Chest Exercises

You should know whether you want to pursue bodybuilding seriously after a few months of weight training. If you're pleased with the outcomes, you're probably hooked. It's exciting to see your body shape up and muscles you didn't know you had. To continue bodybuilding, you must progress to more advanced exercises. The fundamental exercises mentioned in the preceding chapters encompass all the major muscle groups in your upper and lower body, and you can continue to execute them and progress. Even the finest bodybuilders still engage in some of these.

Nevertheless, if you want to excel and set yourself apart from others, you need to expand the variety of your weightlifting exercises. Your muscles can become accustomed to the same exercises if they're done repeatedly, and they will no longer respond. You need to introduce new exercises to your regimen constantly.

Some professionals refer to this as "shocking" the muscles. The goal is to force a muscle to do an unfamiliar activity, which results in new muscle growth. Different exercises target different muscle groups. The Standing Barbell Curl, for example, works the biceps as efficiently as any single exercise, yet it focuses on only a portion of the biceps. The biceps is a complex muscle with multiple sections, like other muscles. You must do exercises that work all muscle areas to achieve maximum development. In this and the following chapters, we'll review various specialized workouts to target specific muscle groups. There's no need to do all of the intermediate exercises we'll go over, at least not on a regular basis. Instead, select the exercises best suited to your body and objectives. Ideally, you'll cycle exercises: pick one that generates results, then go on to another, and so on. Even the most determined bodybuilder might become fatigued by repeating the same exercises—and your muscles can go unchecked. Mixing up your workouts may raise your intensity and make bigger results.

Take note of the description that comes with each practice. Doing them correctly is critical to avoid damage and get the most out of them. Before we get into the intermediate chest workouts, let's go over the chest muscles. This will assist you in understanding how the muscles work and selecting exercises that are appropriate for your needs.

MUSCLES OF THE CHEST

All great bodybuilders have well-developed chests. The pectorals, or chest muscles, are so large and prominent that you can't hide them. A massive chest anchors the upper body and enhances the appearance of your shoulders, arms, and abs. For instance, when you see photos of Arnold Schwarzenegger, his chest grabs your eye. His pectorals, and those of other champs, look like thick slabs of sculpted granite. Compared to other muscles, you can develop chest muscles reasonably quickly. Most people enjoy working the chest because they can easily see and feel the muscles as they lift and enjoy the pump. Pectorals are fan-shaped and cover the upper rib cage, then extend across to the upper arms and up to the collarbone. In the simplest sense, pecs allow you to move your arms across your body. They have four distinct parts: upper, lower, inner, and outer. Each part must be fully developed, defined, and separate from the others to receive high marks in judging. To illustrate the effect of different exercises on your chest muscles, let's single out Bench Press, one of the basic chest exercises. It's outstanding but works mainly in the middle of the chest. However, if Bench Press on an incline or decline bench, you shift the focus to the upper or lower pecs.

An incline bench works the upper chest, and a decline bench the lower. (Some benches are adjustable and can be made flat, as well as inclined and declined. Most gyms, however, have separate, dedicated flat benches, incline benches, and decline benches.) If you don't have access to an incline or decline bench, you can achieve similar results with a flat bench. For instance, you can lower the barbell to your lower chest to develop the lower pecs and to your upper chest to work the upper pecs. You can also change your hand position on the bar. Typically, you perform Bench Presses with your hands slightly more than shoulder-width apart. If you widen your grip by a few inches, you shift effort to the outer pecs. The reverse is also true: If you bring your hands closer, you work the inner pecs more.

Chest exercises fall into two main categories: presses and flys. Presses involve lifting a barbell or dumbbell vertically over your chest (or using a machine that performs the same movement). Flys involve raising and lowering weights horizontally to the sides of your chest. They, too, can be done with free weights or machines. Presses primarily work the center of the pecs from top to bottom, while flys generally target the outside and inside pecs. Some top bodybuilders have built massive chests with only a few exercises, but they are most likely genetically predisposed to having large chest muscles. For most people, variety is critical to good progress.

Here are some key points to remember when doing chest exercises: Be careful. Have a spotter or someone at your side when you use free weights. It's easy to become overconfident in your strength and grab a barbell with too much weight. You may wind up with the barbell on your chest and be unable to move it. That can be scary, as well as embarrassing. You can yell for help, and someone will come to your aid, but it's much more reassuring to have a spotter standing by. Besides helping you if you get in trouble, they can assist you with a final rep or two after you become fatigued. These last few reps, even if assisted, often produce the most remarkable results. You need to warm up. A strained chest muscle can put you out of action for weeks. It can be painful and slow to heal. Fortunately, a strained muscle is easy to avoid with a proper warm-up. This involves doing at least one set with lightweight and more reps than you normally would. A warm-up set loosens your muscles and lets them get the feel of the exercise movement before you move up to heavyweight. A warm-up set can also prepare you mentally.

Barbells, dumbbells, and cables produce slightly different results. With barbells, it's possible to use heavy weights to develop greater mass and strength.

With dumbbells, you can't use as much weight because you're only lifting with one arm at a time. However, dumbbells allow you a more excellent range of motion than barbells, which can be essential in some exercises. Cables attached to weight stacks are standard devices on machines. Like dumbbells, cables provide a wide range of movement. They also allow for a smooth, safe lifting motion.

Keep your chest development in proportion to the rest of your body. Some bodybuilders get fixated on having a massive chest. They do Bench Presses over and over at the expense of exercises for other muscles. The result is an unbalanced physique. It looks somewhat ridiculous to have a bowed-out chest and bird-like arms and legs.

EXERCISES

Upper Pecs Incline Press

Technique: This is identical to Bench Press, described in Chapter 2, except that you lie on an incline bench instead of a flat one. Place your feet on the floor at the end of the bench. With an overhand grip, grab the barbell that's resting on supports above your head, placing your hands slightly more than shoulder-width apart. Raise the bar straight up until it's off the supports. Bring the bar forward until it's directly over your chest, then slowly lower it until the bar touches your chest.

Don't let it bounce off your body. Keep your elbows close to your sides and slightly behind your torso to achieve maximum range of motion. Pause when the bar touches your chest, then lift it straight up, locking your elbows. Repeat.

NOTE: Be sure to keep the weight securely balanced during this exercise. The barbell will have a different balance point when bench pressed on an incline bench than when bench pressed on a level bench. Don't allow your weight to shift back over your head or forward over your abdomen. Start with light weights until you're confident you can raise and lower the weight smoothly and controllably. It's a good idea to start with a spotter. Incline Press is an excellent workout for upper chest development, but you won't be able to utilize as much weight as with Bench Press. You may also do the Incline Press with dumbbells, which allow a slightly longer range of motion than a barbell does. With dumbbells, you start with your palms toward each other, then twist your wrists 90 degrees as you lift so that the palms are oriented toward your feet at the top.

Incline Fly

Technique: This is identical to the Dumbbell Fly, described in earlier chapters, except that you lie on an incline bench. With your hands at your sides, hold a dumbbell in each hand, even with the top of the bench. Extend your arms to the side until your elbows are only slightly bent. Raise the dumbbells upward on a wide path until they are directly over your chest, similar to a hugging motion. Let them touch briefly, then pause. Make sure you have a secure grip, then lower the dumbbells along the same path until they are again even with the top of the bench. Keep your arms bent slightly at the elbow throughout. Repeat.

NOTE: As with the Incline Press, it will take a few sets to get the "feel" of the Incline Fly versus the Dumbbell Fly. Use light weight until you can completely control the dumbbells. Keep them in line over your chest throughout the movement; don't let your arms drift backward so that the dumbbells are over your head or forward so that they are over your abdomen. Your palms should be oriented toward each other throughout the exercise. As with the Dumbbell Fly, don't lower the dumbbells too far to the side on the way down. They should not touch the floor, or you may strain your chest muscles; lower them only to the top of the bench.

Low-Pulley Cable Crossover

Technique: Stand in the middle of two weight stacks, each with a pulley and cable attached. Place your feet slightly wider than shoulder width apart and slightly bend your knees. Cross your arms in front of your body and lean forward until your back is at a 45-degree angle. Take hold of the handles attached to each cable. Pull the cables together with your elbows slightly bent until the handles cross in the center of your chest. Throughout the movement, keep your hands low in front of your knees. Pull the wires as far as they will go, then pause and lower the weights until they touch down gently. Repeat.

NOTE: Keep your back stable during the movement—don't allow your body to move up and down. Maintain steady tension on the cables throughout— don't jerk the weight up and then let it slam down on the stack. Keep your wrists firm. Your palms should be oriented toward each other as they hold the handles throughout the exercise. By keeping your body stable, you focus the effort on your pectorals. Raise and lower the weights at the same speed.

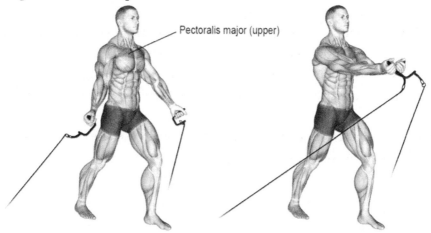

Pectoralis major (upper)

Decline Dumbbell Press

Lower Pecs

Technique: This is identical to the Incline Press with dumbbells, except that you lie on a decline bench, where your legs are higher than your head. By having the bench at this angle, you shift the focus to your lower pectorals. To keep your body stable during the exercise, your knees should be at the end of the bench with your lower legs hanging over the end. There should be a support bar to press your feet against for further stability and to keep you from sliding down. Grab a dumbbell in each hand. Hold them even with the top of the bench, with your arms bent at about a 90-degree angle. Your palms should be oriented toward your feet. Press the dumbbells straight up and slightly in until your elbows lock. Let your elbows extend from your sides for better leverage. Hold, then lower the dumbbells to the starting position. Repeat.

NOTE: It takes a few sets to get acclimated to an incline bench, and it takes time to get used to a decline bench. A decline bench, on the other hand, is highly helpful since it allows you to build your lower pecs significantly better than a flat or incline bench. Make sure your legs are stable at the top of the bench while you complete this exercise—you don't want to slip down the bench. Start with light weight, rising and lowering the dumbbells directly over your lower chest. Don't bounce the dumbbells at the bottom of the movement; doing so will assist you in lifting the dumbbells, reducing efficacy. You won't be able to use as much weight on a decline bench as you can on a flat bench.

Decline Fly

Technique: This is a variant of the Dumbbell Fly, which was discussed in Chapter 2. Allow yourself to become accustomed to the decline bench before using excessive weight. Keep the dumbbells in line over your lower pecs throughout the exercise. Begin with a dumbbell in each hand, your arms slightly bent at the elbows and parallel to the top of the bench. Raise the dumbbells in a wide arc until they rest on your lower pecs. Return them to your sides after a brief pause. Repeat. NOTE: As with all Flye exercises, don't let the dumbbells drop too low at your sides; this could easily strain your chest muscles. Keep your arms slightly bent at the elbows; if you lock them, you make the exercise easier on your pecs.

Bent-Forward Cable Crossover

Technique: This is similar to the Low-Pulley Crossover, described earlier in this chapter. The difference is that you pull the cables together and upward until they cross in front of your chest. With the Low-Pulley Crossover, you keep the cables in front of your thighs. To start this exercise, stand midway between two weight stacks, each of which has a pulley and cable attached. Place your feet slightly more than shoulder-width apart and bend your knees a little. Lean forward only slightly (not at a 45-degree angle, as with the Low-Pulley Crossover). Grab the handles attached to each cable. With your elbows bent slightly, pull the cables together and upward until the handles cross in front of your chest. Keep pulling until your arms form an X and can't go any farther. Hold, then release and slowly lower the weights to the starting position. Repeat.

NOTE: As with the Low-Pulley Crossover, keep your back stable during the movement—don't allow your body to move up and down. Maintain steady tension on the cables throughout— don't jerk the weight up and then let it slam down on the stack. Keep your wrists firm. Your palms should be oriented toward each other as they hold the handles throughout the exercise. In this exercise, feel your pectorals fully flex as your arms cross in front of your chest. Hold that flexed position before you lower the weight. Even as you tire, lower the cables steadily and at the same speed you used to raise them. If done properly, your muscles can get just as much benefit from a "negative" motion (lowering a weight) as from a "positive" motion (raising it).

Cable Fly

Technique: This is identical to the Dumbbell Fly, except that you use cables instead of dumbbells. Place a flat bench midway between two weight stacks. Lie on your back and extend your arms to your sides, grabbing a handle attached to the cable with each hand and with your palms toward each other. As with the Dumbbell Fly, keep your arms bent slightly at the elbow throughout the exercise. Raise and lower the cables directly over your chest in wide arcs. Touch the handles together gently and hold for a second, then lower the weight to the starting position. Be sure to raise both cables at the same speed.

NOTE: Cables provide one benefit over dumbbells: You're able to maintain steady, constant tension throughout the exercise. With dumbbells, it's much more difficult to raise the weight than to lower it. With cables, the effort expended is about the same whether you're raising or lowering the weight. Some bodybuilders believe that cables allow you to "feel" your muscles at work more than dumbbells or barbells do. Many bodybuilders rely on free weights to build bulk and cables to shape and define their muscles, particularly before a contest.

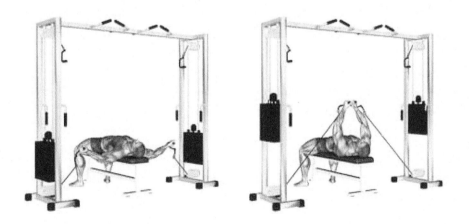

Standing Cable Crossover

Inner Pecs

Technique: The Low-Pulley Cable Crossover and the Bent-Forward Cable Crossover are combined in this workout. The presence of three such comparable workouts demonstrates that minor variations in movement and angle yield drastically diverse results. Top bodybuilders always employ many exercises for the same muscle to work it from head to toe. The Standing Cable Crossover differs from the other two crossover workouts in one important way: Instead of a floor-level pulley, you use a machine with wires attached to an overhead pulley. As a result, instead of pulling the cables up from around your ankles, you're dragging them down from above your head.

With this motion, you work your inner pecs more. Here are the key differences between these cable exercises:

- Low-Pulley Cable Crossover: Your back is bent at a 45-degree angle. You cross the handles in front of your thighs.

- Bent-Forward Cable Crossover: Your back is bent forward only slightly, at about a 10- to 15-degree angle. You cross the handles in front of your chest.

- Standing Cable Crossover: Your back is bent at about a 30-degree angle. You cross the handles in front of your waist.

NOTE: With the Standing Cable Crossover, you must tilt your entire body forward, from your feet to your head. This enables you to maintain your balance when raising and lowering the wires from the high pulleys. In this exercise, like in the others, do not stop pulling until the handles touch in front of your body; instead, continue pulling until your arms can no longer go any farther. This additional motion provides the most muscle benefit. To provide variety, switch how your hands cross with each rep, allowing your right hand to be in front on one rep and your left hand to be in front on the next.

Flat Bench Cable Crossover

Technique: Another part of your pecs is targeted by this cable crossover workout. You are not required to accomplish all of these crossovers, but we are providing them for variety. Certain activities are more comfortable and beneficial for people than others. This activity is self-explanatory. Place a flat bench between two weight stacks with pulleys at the floor level. Lie down on the bench on your back. Grab the cables' handles with your palms up and straighten your arms out to the sides, virtually locking your elbows. Bring the cables together across your chest so that the grips barely touch. Hold the weight, then lower it until your hands are level with the top of the bench.

NOTE: Lift the cables slightly past the point where the handles touch as an alternative. This causes your pecs to contract even more, which is the purpose of all weightlifting workouts. Throughout the movement, keep your back flat on the bench. Avoid the urge to arch your back (which would make it easier to lift the weight but would reduce the effort by the pecs). Never jerk the cables up and then let them fall, as with other cable exercises. Raise and drop the weights in a smooth, progressive manner. The downward motion can be just as beneficial as the upward, if done properly.

Machine Fly

Technique: This exercise has a similar impact as the Dumbbell Fle. The distinction is that you use equipment known as a "pec deck," which is typically found in gyms. Lean against the seat back as you sit. (You can modify the seat height to suit your needs.) Extend your arms to the side and make a 90-degree bend in your elbows so that your upper arms are parallel to the floor. Place your forearms, shoulder-width apart and as high as your collarbone, against two pads fastened to bars. Push the pads together until they meet in front of your nose. You elevate a weight stack behind your back by squeezing the pads together. Hold, then let the pads separate and return to the starting position. Repeat.

NOTE: Maintain a flat back against the seat back. Reduce the weights to 2 or 3 inches above the stack. This puts your muscles under constant tension—you don't rest when the weights strike the stack. Furthermore, it enables for a more fluid start to the lifting motion. If you let the weights fall to the stack, your pecs may strain as they extend too far to the sides. Exercises on this machine will not build the pectoral mass and growth that free weights can. The pec deck, on the other hand, can be highly beneficial in terms of building definition and shape in your chest. Wrap your fingers over the tops of the pads for more control during the workout.

Narrow-Grip Bench Press

Technique: The bench press is one of the most fundamental chest workouts. On a barbell, your hands should be somewhat wider than shoulder width apart, but for this exercise, utilize a narrow grip with your hands just around 12 inches apart. The emphasis is now on your inner pecs. You won't be able to lift nearly as much weight with this grip as you would with a standard, wider grip. (With a narrow grip, your full pecs do not participate in lifting.) The raising and lowering movement is the same as for a conventional Bench Press. Lie on your back on a flat bench, knees at the end of the bench, feet on the floor. Lift the barbell off the supports overhead. Carefully bring the barbell forward until it's directly over your chest, then lower it straight down until it barely touches your chest. Push up until your arms lock. Allow your elbows to flare to the side for greater support and leverage.

NOTE: If performed wrong, this exercise might be hazardous. You don't have nearly as much control of the bar with a narrow grip as you do with a wider grasp. First and foremost, use significantly less weight than you would for a typical Bench Press. Take extra caution when removing the barbell from the support and bringing it forward to begin the lifting process. When performing Narrow-Grip Bench Press, always employ a spotter. As you weary, it's simple for the bar to become unstable and collapse to one side or the other, potentially hurting you or someone else. If you become comfortable with your hands only 12 inches apart on the bar, you can experiment with moving them closer. The closer together they are, the more your inner pecs will be worked. Be extremely careful—the narrower the grip, the more difficult it is to balance and lift the weight.

Flat Bench Dumbbell Press

Outer Pecs

Technique: This is a version of the Bench Press. Lie on a flat bench with a dumbbell in each hand at your sides, palms down. Extend your arms away from your body and make a 90-degree bend in your elbows. Lift the dumbbells up straight until your elbows lock. The weights should be about 6 inches apart at the top. Hold for a second, then return to the starting position at your side. Repeat.

NOTE: Instead of putting your feet on the floor, try putting them on top of the bench. This prevents you from "cheating" with your legs by utilizing them to assist you in lifting the dumbbells. With your feet on the bench, your chest muscles become isolated. For more variety, you can rotate your wrists 90 degrees inward as you lift so that your palms are oriented toward each other at the top of the motion. Then you can rotate your wrists back as you lower the weight so that they're in the starting position again

Dips

Technique: This was one of the fundamental exercises covered in Chapter 2. It does not employ weights; instead, your own body provides all resistance. Dips are one of the most effective chest exercises. Almost every gym has "dip bars," which are freestanding, parallel bars about chest high and somewhat wider than shoulder width apart. Place yourself between the bars. Raise your toes and place your palms on the bars. Exhale, then straighten your arms and raise your body until your elbows lock. Your feet should be about a foot off the ground, and your waist should be parallel to the top of the bars. Hold for a second, then inhale and lower yourself gradually to the starting position, with your chest even with the bars. Bend your knees slightly to keep your feet from touching the floor. You may want to cross your ankles to keep your legs still. At the bottom, hold for a second, then exhale and push yourself back up until your elbows lock.

NOTE: Maintain a tiny forward lean in your torso for greater balance. The more forward you can lean (while maintaining your balance), the more your outside pecs are worked. You'll naturally lean forward more if you lift your ankles toward your buttocks. If you drop yourself too much on the bars at initially, you may hurt your shoulders. The lower you can go safely, though, the more your outside pecs will benefit. Some dip bars are parallel to one another, whereas others feature horizontal bars that taper at one end. Experiment with different hand placements if you utilize the latter. If you do Dips where the bars are farther apart, your outer pecs will get more work. If the bars are closer together, the effort shifts to your inner pecs. Advanced bodybuilders sometimes attach weights to their waist for greater resistance. Don't try this until you are very comfortable with regular Dips.

Wide-Grip Incline Press

Technique: The Narrow-Grip Bench Press, as previously mentioned, works the inside pecs. In this exercise, on the other hand, you widen your hand position to train the outside pecs more thoroughly. Put your hands as close to the ends of the bar as seems natural. If you feel yourself straining, bring them closer. With a broad grasp, you won't be able to lift as much weight as you would with a regular, shoulder-width grip.

NOTE: Just as with the Narrow-Grip Bench Press, use light weight initially; otherwise, you can easily strain your pecs. Have a spotter nearby and wear a belt to support your back. Let your elbows flare to the sides as you lift for more control. Keep your back flat against the bench. Be sure to keep the barbell balanced as you raise and lower the weight.

Intermediate Shoulder Exercises

The deltoids are important glenohumeral joint stabilizers that must be strong and coordinated to move swiftly and prevent shoulder dislocations. The deltoids have three heads, each of which serves a specific purpose. When you're skinny enough, you'll be able to see the three heads contracting when training. A well-developed middle head, or lateral deltoid, is the subdivision of the delts that leads to the illusion of the wide X shape stated previously. The anterior head is in front of the body, whereas the posterior head is in the back. The anterior head is addressed during push-up variations because it is a strong shoulder flexor and transverse, or horizontal, adductor. (Adduction moves a limb toward the body's midline, and abduction moves a limb away from the body's midline.) The posterior head is worked during various rowing and pull-up exercises because it acts as a shoulder extensor and transverse, or horizontal, abductor. However, this head is often underdeveloped. Specific attention to the rear delts is usually provided through transverse abduction movements of the shoulder. While all three heads contribute to handstand push-up movements, the anterior and lateral heads are worked the most during this category of lifts. The posterior head keeps the shoulder stable and contributes slightly to the overall motion. Even if you never targeted your deltoids, you may develop a lot through horizontal pressing and pulling motions like push-ups and inverted rows. You must work with them to take your delt development to the next level. Many years ago, when overhead pressing was more prevalent than horizontal pressing, there appeared to be fewer shoulder problems. This exercise resulted in more solid shoulder muscles and more balanced strength levels. It should be no surprise that the deltoids play an essential role in athletic motions.

We mentioned in the last chapter that all great bodybuilders had massive chests. The same is true for the shoulders. A broad, massive chest goes well with broad, massive shoulders.

Shoulders are the foundation for the acute V form that distinguishes a great bodybuilder—a broad upper body shrinking to a narrow waist. Some people are born with broad shoulders, while others must work hard to earn them. The deltoids, or "delts," are the shoulder muscles. They are huge, spherical muscles located at the ends of our shoulder bones. Delts are located slightly above the triceps (upper arm muscles) and connect to the chest muscles (pecs). Delts also join the trapezius muscles (traps) of the upper back. We include traps in our discussion of shoulder muscles because most bodybuilders exercise their delts and traps at the same time. The traps are flat, triangle-shaped muscles that start at the base of the neck in the back and extend across the shoulder blades, then down to the middle of the back. The top of the traps can be seen from the front of the body, connecting the shoulder muscles to the neck.

The deltoid is considered one muscle but has three distinct parts or heads. All three heads must be fully grown for the shoulders to be regarded as excellent. The anterior head of the deltoid is in the front, the medial head is on the side, and the posterior head is at the back. It is critical to understand the role of each component in daily operations. We can elevate our arms to the front of our body thanks to the anterior head. We can lift our arms to the sides thanks to the medial head. The posterior head allows us to raise our arms behind our bodies, much like a sprinter does to grab a baton during a race.

All three heads function together when you extend your arms straight out from your sides and rotate them in a circle. Some shoulder exercises work all three deltoid parts in varying degrees, but most exercises target one head more than the others. We'll describe exercises that work all three. Most people tend to work the front head most because it's the most visible, but you can't ignore the side and back heads if you want to be competitive in a bodybuilding contest. Muscle proportion is critical in bodybuilding. If you develop one muscle—or a part of one muscle—more than those around it, your physique is flawed. As you gain experience, pay attention to which areas seem to develop faster than others to adjust your regimen as necessary.

152

Remember that poor shoulder growth cannot be concealed in competition. Almost every stance shows at least one component of the deltoid. Poses intended to show off chest muscles, for example, emphasize the front delts. Back poses highlight the back delts. Side poses highlight the side delts. You must develop the entire deltoid area distinct from the pecs and traps. Again, definition is essential in bodybuilding. Some people are born with greater separation between their delts and surrounding muscles, whereas others must work harder to obtain it. Well-developed delts give you more than a broad look; they give you a thick look. Thickness, or hardness, is another essential element in bodybuilding. People often develop broad shoulders soon after they begin serious weight training, but thickness is more complicated and takes longer to achieve.

Thickness distinguishes bodybuilding champions from "want to bes." We discussed the need for warm-up sets earlier in this book to avoid straining muscles. Use lighter weights (approximately half of what you would use for training) and perform twice as many reps. Warm-up sets are critical while working on your shoulders since lifting too much weight too quickly can cause injury. A strained shoulder might take a long time to heal, causing chronic issues that may force you to miss workouts. Warm-up sets of a few minutes can go a long way toward preventing shoulder problems. You can do warm-ups with any of the exercises listed below. Use light weight and proper form to get the best possible warm-up. Delts can be slow to develop. For most people, they don't grow as quickly as pecs or biceps. You need to be patient and stick with the exercises. Some bodybuilding champs worked long and hard before their delts became respectable. The deltoid muscles are complicated since they move your arms in a circle to the front, rear, and side.

A number of workouts are required to work the entire deltoid area. Deltoid workouts are classified into two types: presses and rises. Presses involve lifting weight directly above your head.

Presses involve all three delt heads. Lifting the weight in a wide arc to the front, side, or rear of your body is what rises are all about. Front raises help to strengthen the front head, side raises help to strengthen the medial head, and back raises help to strengthen the posterior head. With raises, especially, the amount of weight you use is far less important than lifting with proper form. You want to isolate the delts as you lift without drawing on the strength of your back or legs. "Many bodybuilders try to go too heavy when they train delts," said Steve Brisbois, a former leading bodybuilder. "The delts are small muscles and don't require tons of weight to grow, but they require high-intensity work and strict form to keep the leverage on the shoulders. I use a weight heavy enough to tax the muscle but light enough to control."

EXERCISES

Front Delts Military Press

Technique: Bend your knees, lower your buttocks, and grab a barbell with an overhand hold from the floor (palms down, thumbs in). Your hands and feet should be about shoulder-width apart. Standing, slowly bring the bar to your shoulders, aligning it with your collarbone. Your palms should be under the bar for stability, and your elbows should be close to your sides. Hold the barbell for a second, then gently raise it straight up toward your face until your elbows lock. Maintain a healthy and balanced weight. Take care not to lean back or front. Hold for a moment at the peak, then lower the bar to your shoulders without bouncing it against your chest. Repeat.

Note: Instead of lifting a barbell off the floor, utilize one from a shoulder-high rack for this exercise. Bringing the bar to the beginning position at your shoulders, this will assist prevent lower back strain. Military Press can also be performed while sitting, which isolates your delts even more and stops you from "cheating" with your legs. Military Press benches are uniquely built with a flat seat and a short back to help support your body as you lift. Other equipment allows you to perform a Military Press lifting motion. Always wear a belt when doing any variation of this exercise, which can place a large amount of stress on your lower back. Military Press is the most basic exercise for front delt development but also works the side delts.

Dumbbell Press

Technique: Dumbbell Press is the same as Military Press, except it is performed with dumbbells rather than a barbell. Dumbbell Press is best performed while seated to avoid wobbling. As you lift, allow your elbows to flare out to the sides to help balance the weight. You can raise the dumbbells one at a time or all at once. Some bodybuilders believe that lifting each arm independently results in a more fluid, smooth motion. Try both ways and decide which one you prefer.

Note: Wear a belt during Dumbbell Press to protect your lower back. Dumbbell presses have two advantages over barbell presses: Because there is no bar in the middle to hit your chest, you can lower the weight further and change the distance between your hands at the peak of the exercise. You can, for example, draw the dumbbells together until they touch at the top, or you can have them shoulder-width apart. Alternatively, you can keep your palms facing forward while you progressively lift or rotate your wrists so that your palms face each other at the top.

Arnold Press

Technique: There are some fundamental differences between Arnold Press and Dumbbell Press. Begin with the dumbbells at shoulder height, palms inward rather than outward. Rotate your wrists 90 degrees as you lift so that your palms are facing forward at the top. At the top, do not lock your elbows. Rotate your wrists back so that your palms are pointed inward when you descend the dumbbells.

NOTE: Arnold Press is named for Arnold Schwarzenegger, who popularized it. It's best done while seated for greater upper body stability. For variety, you can lower the dumbbells to your chest instead of stopping at your shoulders. This increases the range of motion and works the delts in a slightly different way.

Front Dumbbell Raise

Technique: The Front Dumbbell Raise can be performed standing or sitting. Hold dumbbells at your sides, thumbs pointing in opposite directions. Straighten your left arm and raise it in front of and overhead of your body. Pause at the peak, then slowly descend the dumbbell while simultaneously elevating your right arm. Both arms should be moving in front of your face at the same time. Keep your arms parallel to one another and your torso stable. Bend your knees slightly if performing the Front Dumbbell Raise while standing.

NOTE: When lifting, you can keep your wrists in line with your forearms or gently bend your wrists down. You can also rotate your wrists 90 degrees so that the dumbbells are held vertically rather than horizontally. Some bodybuilders believe that carrying them this manner reduces strain on the shoulder joint. You can also use a barbell instead of dumbbells to achieve this lifting motion. Maintain a straight arm and an overhand grip. Raise the bar gradually in front of your body, then to your brow, but not all the way overhead.

Clean and Press

Technique: The term "clean" refers to the motion of lifting the barbell off the floor and to a resting position in front of your chest. The weight is then "pressed" or lifted overhead. You return the barbell to the floor after each repetition. This is how it differs from the Military Press, in which you begin and conclude each rep with the bar at your shoulders. Lowering yourself to the ground for each rep in order to "clean" the weight can be taxing on your lower back. To do it safely, use the following method: Squat with your knees fully bent and your thighs parallel to the floor. Lean forward slightly and grab the bar with an overhand grip and with your hands shoulder-width apart. With a smooth, steady motion, stand and lift the barbell at the same time. Bring it to the top of your chest, even with your shoulders. Pause, then lift the weight overhead under control. Pause again, then lower the bar to your chest, bend your knees, and place the barbell back on the floor—in one continuous motion.

NOTE: Because of all the squatting and standing with Clean and Press, use extreme caution. If it continues to be awkward or painful, don't do it; there are other exercises that can produce the same results. However, some advanced bodybuilders swear by Clean and Press. They've learned to do it properly, and they say it produces thick, hard deltoids—while developing your traps, arms, and back as well. It's considered a "holistic" exercise.

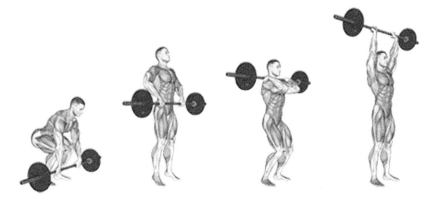

Side Delts Dumbbell Lateral Raise

Technique: Stand shoulder-width apart with your feet shoulder-width apart and a dumbbell in each hand at your sides. Bend forward at the waist slightly. Raise your arms slowly from your sides, elbows slightly bent. Rotate your wrists down slightly as you lift, so that the back of the dumbbell is higher than the front. Lift until the dumbbells are just above your shoulders. Don't rock your body. Hold the weights for a second over your shoulders, then slowly drop them to the beginning position at your side. Begin each new rep by coming to a complete stop and not swinging the weight up. Keep your torso stable, maintaining a slight forward lean.

NOTE: You can do this exercise seated if you have trouble keeping your upper body stationary. If you do it properly, you should feel a slight burning sensation in the side delt. That's a good sign. Wear a belt to ease the strain on your lower back. For variety, you can bring the dumbbells down toward the front of your body instead of to the side. In addition, you can bend your elbows at a 90-degree angle instead of keeping your arms straight.

Cable Lateral Raise

Technique: The Cable Lateral Raise is very similar to the Dumbbell Lateral Raise, except that you use a machine with a cable. Cables provide the advantage of continuous, steady tension as you raise and lower the weight. Unlike the Dumbbell Lateral Raise, you work one arm at a time with the Cable Lateral Raise. Stand with the right side of your body about a foot from the weight stack. Grab the handle with your left hand, so that your left arm crosses in front of your chest.

For stability, bend your right arm and lay your right hand on your hip. Pull the wire out and up with your left elbow bent until your left hand is higher than your shoulder. As you lift, gently twist the front of your wrist down (as if pouring water from a pitcher). When you finish the reps, stand about a foot away from the weight stack on your left side. Lift the cord with your right hand like you would your left.

NOTE: Don't let your body sway while lifting. Use only your deltoid. As you lower the weight, let the handle drop slightly below the middle of your torso. Let the weights touch down only slightly before lifting again. You can also lift while sitting. For more variety, you can step forward a few inches and lift the cable behind your body instead of in front.

 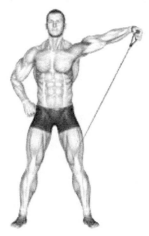

Lying Side Lateral

Technique: The Lying Side Lateral combines elements of the Dumbbell Lateral Raise and the Cable Lateral Raise. Lie on a bench (either flat or incline) on your right side. Hold a dumbbell in your left hand near or slightly below your hip. Your elbow should be slightly bent. Lower the dumbbell in front of your body until it's about 6 inches from the floor.

Pause, then lift your arm straight up until it's directly overhead. The front of the dumbbell should point down slightly or be parallel to the floor. When you finish the reps, turn and lie on your right side. Repeat the exercise with your right hand.

NOTE: Use light weight so that you can perform the motion properly. By lying on a bench instead of the floor, you have a greater range of motion.

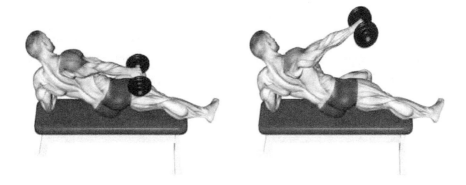

Prone Dumbbell Lateral Raise

Technique: Lie face down on an incline bench with your head at the top. Grab a dumbbell in each hand and let your arms hang loosely down with your palms oriented toward each another. Bend your elbows slightly and raise the dumbbells away from your sides and upward in a wide arc. Stop when the weights are just above your shoulders. Lift gradually and under control. As you near the top, turn the front of the dumbbells down slightly to focus effort on the side delt. At the top, hold the dumbbell for a moment, then lower it along the same path until it's about 2 inches below the bench.

Bent-Over Dumbbell Lateral Raise

Rear Delts

Technique: Do this exercise while seated. It's identical to the Dumbbell Lateral Raise, described above, except that you bend forward at the waist at about a 45-degree angle to work the back part of the delt.

NOTE: Keep in mind the following points:

1. Sit with your feet close together and your knees almost touching.
2. Start with the dumbbells behind your calves and return them there, until they almost touch.
3. Don't raise your body as you lift—this would reduce the benefit to your delts.
4. Raise the dumbbells just above head high.
5. Keep the dumbbells in line with your shoulders throughout the movement, with your palms oriented toward each other. Don't let the dumbbells drift behind your shoulders.
6. At the top of the movement, pause, then lower the dumbbells under control.

Bent-Over Cable Lateral Raise

Technique: This is a variation on the Cable Lateral Raise. The main distinction is that the Bent-Over Cable Lateral Raise employs two cables rather than one, and you lift with both arms at the same time. Stand shoulder-width apart, midway between two weight stacks. Cross your arms in an X in front of your body and hold the handles. The handle on your right side will be held by your left hand, and the handle on your left side will be held by your right hand. Bend your knees until your back is nearly parallel to the floor. Pull your arms out and up in a broad, fluid motion until they are above your head. Pause, then let the weights lower and your hands cross in front of your body.

NOTE: You should feel continuous, steady tension on your rear delts throughout this exercise. Don't raise your torso; keep it almost parallel to the floor—this keeps the effort on the rear delt.

Bent-Over Row

Technique: Grab a barbell with an overhand grip and your hands 8 to 10 inches apart. Stand with your feet slightly more than shoulder-width apart. Bend your torso forward at a 45-degree angle. Keeping your legs and upper body stationary, lift the barbell straight up until it touches the top of your abs. Hold momentarily, then lower it under control, stopping in front of your shins.

NOTE: A similar exercise, the Upright Row, is a classic for lat and trap development. By bending your torso forward, you shift the effort to your rear delts. Be sure to lift the barbell only as high as your upper abs—not all the way neck. Wear a belt to protect your lower back. Prone Dumbbell Lateral Raise Technique: Sit at the end of a flat bench. Place your feet close together on the floor. Lean over until your torso rests against your thighs. Holding a dumbbell in each hand, let your arms hang straight down with your palms oriented toward each other. Bend your elbows slightly, then lift the dumbbells up and out, keeping them in line with your shoulders. Stop when the weights reach head high. Pause, then lower the dumbbells gradually to the starting position.

NOTE: Keep your torso stationary during the movement. For variety, you can raise the dumbbells a little to the front of your shoulders, instead of in line with them.

Upright Row

Traps

Technique: Grab a barbell with an overhand grip and your hands 8 to 10 inches apart. Stand with your feet slightly more than shoulder-width apart and the barbell resting against the front of your body. Keep your legs stationary and your back straight. Lift the barbell straight up—keeping it close to your torso—until it almost touches your chin. Hold momentarily, then lower it under control to a position just below your waist.

NOTE: Keep your head up and your eyes looking forward throughout the exercise. This isolates your traps instead of allowing your entire torso to lift the weight. Wear a belt to stabilize your lower back.

Shrugs

Technique: Grab a barbell with an overhand grip and your hands shoulder-width apart. Let the bar rest against your thighs. Lift or "shrug" your shoulders as high as you can, as if they are going to touch your ears. Keep your lower body steady and arms bent slightly at the elbows. Don't sway. When your shoulders are at the highest point, pause momentarily, then gradually lower your shoulders and the bar to the starting position.

NOTE: This is a very short movement. The bar rises only 4 to 6 inches as you shrug your shoulders. The distance is not important—proper form is. Your traps can get a great workout with very little movement. As you lift, dip your chin toward your chest slightly. This helps stabilize your torso and focuses the effort on the traps instead of the chest or delts. You can try a wider or narrower grip to work different areas of the traps. Wear a belt to protect your lower back. Shrugs can also be done with dumbbells. However, hold them at your sides, not in front. Let your arms hang straight down throughout the motion. Some people find this exercise more comfortable and effective with dumbbells because they allow you to have a longer range of motion.

Lying Incline Lateral

Technique: Place your head at the top of an incline bench, facing down. With your hands facing each other, hold a dumbbell in each hand. Allow your arms to hang loosely. Bend your elbows slightly, then raise your arms in a wide arc above and in front of your shoulders. They should be parallel to your ears. To fully train the traps, twist the front of the dumbbells down slightly at the top. Hold for a second before lowering the dumbbells to the starting position.

NOTE: In the first part of this exercise, your delts will do most of the work. As your arms approach the topmost position, your traps come into play. At the very highest point, you should feel your traps fully contract. Be sure to keep the dumbbells in line with your ears, not back a few inches (in line with your shoulder joints). That small difference causes your traps to work more than your delts.

T-Bar Row

Technique: This exercise is similar to the Upright Row, except that you don't use a barbell. Instead, you use a piece of equipment that has a long metal bar (longer than a barbell), with one end hinged at the floor. Place weights on the free end. Step onto a wooden box or platform and straddle the bar. Bend your knees slightly, lean over and grab a short bar that forms a T with the long bar. Pull the weights toward your chest. Keep your back bent at a 45-degree angle. Lift until the weights touch your chest. Pause, then lower the weights, straightening your arms.

NOTE: Keep your head up and your eyes looking forward during the T-Bar Row to ease the strain on your neck. Pull your shoulders back slightly as you lift. Don't let your body sway. If you can't remain stationary, you're using too much weight; remove some weight until you can lift with proper form.

Back and Neck Exercises

"Thick" and "wide"—are the two words most commonly used to describe outstanding back development. An awe-inspiring back can be the final piece of the puzzle needed to achieve bodybuilding success. Too often, young bodybuilders—and even seasoned veterans—overlook the back in their workouts. The reason is simple. Bodybuilding judges, as well as others, tend to notice a person's chest and shoulders first. A trained eye is required to appreciate the less visible, less dramatic set of muscles that comprise the back. However, a broad back is essential for achieving bodybuilders' severe V form—an expansive upper torso that tapers to a tiny waist. Well-developed "lats," or the muscles that protrude from the sides of the torso, are readily visible from the front and play an important part in many obligatory competition poses. Don't devote so much time and effort to the "showy" muscles (chest, shoulders, biceps, and legs) that you don't have time to train the back adequately. Some people become discouraged because back muscles often develop more slowly than other muscles, which seem to pop out quickly with serious training. A championship-caliber back may require years of focused preparation. As a beginner bodybuilder, you should commit to training your back as seriously as any other body region. Don't be concerned if you don't see immediate benefits. You'll improve if you do the right exercises with the proper form, even if the payoff is a little further down the line. Making your back a priority from the start can help you avoid an issue that some advanced bodybuilders face. They advance to the top of the sport only to discover that their undeveloped backs prevent them from becoming champions.

MUSCLES OF THE BACK

Before you can hope to sculpt a massive, "ripped" back, you have to understand the muscles that comprise it. Simply saying "back muscles" is too general and too oversimplified to be helpful. Unless you understand each muscle and its function, you can't target it with specific exercises.

Latissimus Dorsi

The "lats" are the triangle-shaped muscles that run from below the armpits to the lower back on both sides. They are the biggest muscles in the back and the only ones visible from a frontal perspective. When bodybuilders are relaxed, their lats are often not visible. When the lats are flexed, they spread out like wings under the arms. People who do not do weights have little lat development. Therefore when you see someone with large lats, you know they're a bodybuilder. Lat muscular strength isn't simply for show. They let you pull your arms backward and allow you to lift and carry heavy weight without straining your lower back. To develop great lats, you need to do exercises with a pulldown movement, such as Chin-Ups. Another exercise is the Cable Pulldown—you grab a long bar overhead and press it down toward the floor, raising a weight stack. You can work different areas of the lats by varying the grip and the lifting motion when doing the exercises. For example, doing the Cable Pulldown with the bar in front of your head yields one result. If you pull the bar behind your head, you'll obtain another. Over the years, innovations in training methods have contributed to more significant and better back growth. Consider today's bodybuilding superstars, whose backs dwarf top competitors from decades ago. The upper and lower lats are separated. Lower lats extend from the center of the back almost to the waist. You'll do exercises with a limited grasp to strengthen them. When your hands are close together, chin-ups and cable pulldowns are good. These similar workouts and many others strengthen the upper lats by employing a considerably wider grip.

174

Upper Back

The trapezius muscles, or "traps," are the muscles in the upper and middle region of the back. They are flat and triangular, stretching horizontally across the shoulder blades and vertically down to the middle of the spine from the base of the neck. Traps allow you to raise and lower your shoulders. Although the traps are technically back muscles, bodybuilders train them with shoulder muscles. In the last chapter, we covered many trap exercises, such as Shrugs and Upright Rows. If necessary, go through them again. Traps that are well-developed offer a clean center line to your back, highlighting large lats on either side. Your traps must be well-defined and distinctly separate from your lats.

Middle Back

Of all the back muscles, those of the middle back may be the most ignored. You can easily spot wing-like lats and tall traps, but the middle back muscles often get lost in the mix. They are subtle, yet they must become thick and prominent to complete your back development. Someone who does not have a good middle back will pale compared to someone who does, although you may not immediately be able to identify why. Judges, however, are trained to spot every flaw, and their eyes quickly go to the middle back when sizing up competitors. To develop the muscles of the middle back, you need to do exercises that involve an extended range of motion. Extreme pulling and stretching movements call the middle back muscles into action.

A good example is the Cable Row. You sit on the floor (or on a seat) facing a weight stack and pull two cables toward your chest. The exercise requires you to fully straighten and extend your arms as you return the weight, then pull your arms as far back as possible to lift the weight.

Lower back An outstanding lower back is marked by two thick vertical columns of muscles on either side of the lower spine called spinal erectors. They start about 4 inches above your waist and extend below your waistline. Spinal erectors help you to arch your spine to perform many day-to-day functions. They stabilize your lower torso and protect your spine from injury. They don't flex dramatically, like biceps or lats. Although they tend to keep their shape whether you're relaxing or working out, they must be prominent if you are to have a fully developed back. Spinal erectors can quickly become strained or seriously injured by improper lifting or too much work. Yet they are critical in helping to avoid lower back problems, which are familiar to many people. The more you develop these muscles, the less likely you are to develop these back problems. When you begin to work your lower back, warm up thoroughly and proceed carefully. Given their small size, you don't need much weight to build your spinal erectors. Proper form is much more critical. Bring these muscles along slowly as you sculpt your entire physique, but ensure you don't ignore them. They can become a weak link in your back development if you don't target them in training.

BACK EXERCISES

Lats Lat Pulldown

Technique: This exercise is done on a machine found in almost every gym. A long horizontal overhead bar is attached to a cable that ties into a stack of weights. Crouch down on your knees under the bar or sit on a seat if one is provided. Raise your arms overhead and grab the bar with a wide overhand grip—about 2 to 3 inches from the ends. Angle your torso slightly and pull the bar down smoothly in front of your face until it touches the top of your chest. Hold for a second, then gradually let the bar rise to its starting position.

Note:

Keep your torso steady.

Don't let your torso sway backward—doing so takes effort off the lats and shifts it to the upper back. When your torso is steady, the lats do all the pulling.

If you have trouble remaining stationary, have a spotter gently place their hands on your shoulders.

Keep steady tension on the weights as you return them to the starting position.

Don't let go of the bar and let the weights slam down. You should keep the same tension on the cable as you lift and lower the weights.

Some lat machines have a short, inverted V-shaped handle instead of a long bar. To use this type of handle, grasp both sides of the V and perform the exercise as with the straight bar. Because you're using a much narrower grip, your lower lats will get more of a workout. If your gym doesn't have a V handle, you can accomplish the same result by bringing your hands closer together on a straight bar. On a straight bar, you can also experiment with an underhand grip (palms up, thumbs out).

Machine Pullover

Technique: This exercise is also performed on a machine found in most gyms. You begin by sitting on a seat that has a back. Above your head is a large U-shaped bar, with the open part of the U facing out. Place your elbows on the two pads at the open end. Press down firmly on the pads with your upper arms, lowering the U-shaped bar toward your chest. Stop when it touches your abs.

Note: The bar moves in a semicircular motion from start to finish. While pressing down on the bar, you can wrap your fingers around the top of the bar for a firmer hold. Keep your back firmly against the back of the seat. If a pullover machine is not available in your gym, you can do essentially the same exercise with a barbell. Start lying on a flat bench with your head slightly off one end. Grab a barbell and hold it behind your head off the floor. Bend your arms at a 90-degree angle and keep them close to your sides. Smoothly lift the barbell over your head and toward your chest, stopping when it touches your chest. You may want a spotter to press down gently on your thighs, so your body doesn't rise off the bench. A word of caution: If you're using a high bench, don't try to reach behind and grab a barbell off the floor. You can strain your lats doing so. Instead, have someone hand you the barbell.

One-Arm Cable Row

Technique:
Use a machine with a pulley on the floor.
Grab the handle with your right hand when sitting or standing (thumb up). Pull the cable toward your right side, pausing when the handle comes into contact with your ribcage. Your elbow should be a reasonable distance behind your torso.
For superior balance when pulling the rope while standing, place your feet even or with your left foot firmly in front of your right. For added support, if you complete this exercise while seated, place your left forearm on your left knee. After you've completed the reps, switch sides and pull with your left hand.

Note: This exercise is particularly effective in developing your upper lats. Because of the long range of motion from start to finish, you get more benefits than most other exercises. For variety, you can gradually twist the handle toward your torso as you lift so that your thumb is at your side when you finish.

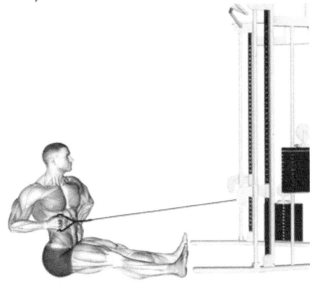

Chin-Ups

Technique: This flexible exercise, like Dips, does not need weights; your body provides all of the resistance. This is an activity that many of us remember from gym class in elementary school. You stand beneath a horizontal bar that is a few inches to a foot or more above your head. Raise your arms high and take a broad overhand grip on the bar (palms down, thumbs in). Your hands should be slightly wider apart than shoulder width. Make a tight grasp on the bar and raise your body up until your upper chest hits it and your chin is above it. Bend your knees and cross your ankles as you go to maintain your lower body stable. Keep your elbows behind your torso as you lift. At the topmost position, hold for a second, then lower yourself to the starting position.

NOTE:

Chin-Ups are difficult for some people, especially those who are overweight. You might not even be able to execute a single chin-up at first. If this is the case, skip this exercise until you have gained strength through other exercises, and then attempt it again. Try to straighten your arms almost completely as you lower yourself if you can execute Chin-Ups. This stretches your lats nicely. Keep your lats flexed as you hang so that your shoulder joints don't bear all of your body weight. You can change the width or narrowness of your grip to add diversity. The wider the grip, the more upper lats you work. If you're especially strong, you can put your head in front of the bar (instead of behind) and lift until the back of your neck touches the bar (instead of your chin touching the bar). Some advanced bodybuilders attach weights to their waist to increase the resistance. A word of caution: If you're using a bar that's much higher than your head, be careful as you reach for it to start the exercise—either stand on a stool or have someone assist you as you jump up to grab the bar.

Seated Cable Row

Middle Back

Technique: The Seated Cable Row is similar to the One-Arm Cable Row described above for lats. The primary differences are that you pull with two hands at the same time and that you are seated rather than standing. Use a machine with a pulley on the floor. Sitting on or near the floor, slightly bend your knees and place your feet against a horizontal bar for support. Take hold of the V-shaped grip with your thumbs up. Pull the cable toward your ribcage by leaning back slightly. Draw your shoulder blades together and arch your back slightly. Maintain a close grip on your arms. Stop when the handles hit your abdomen; your elbows should be well behind your torso at this point. Hold for a few seconds, then gradually return the weights to their starting position. Some machines have two cables and two handles. With others, a single cable splits into two short cables that are connected to one handle. With either type, the lifting motion is the same.

NOTE: The range of motion for this exercise is less than that of the One-Arm Cable Row. As a result, it works the middle back more than the lats, though the lats benefit as well. Lean back slightly while you pull the cables, but then straighten your torso at the conclusion. This allows your back muscles to do more work than your lats. When you lower the weight, make sure to fully extend your arms and lean forward to stretch your lats. To provide diversity, gradually rotate the handle toward your body as you raise until your thumb is at your side.

Advance Arm Exercises

If you poll top bodybuilders, you will find that they all have different motives for getting into the sport. They all obviously wanted to better their physiques and create bigger muscles in general. Most bodybuilders are first obsessed with large arms, specifically biceps. Biceps, or "guns," as they're commonly referred as, stand out like no other muscular group. Big biceps express strength, power, and authority. The muscles of the chest, shoulders, stomach, and legs can be disguised under a bodybuilder's attire, but huge biceps stick out like two mountain peaks, especially when paired with a short-sleeved shirt. Some beginning weight lifters care only about biceps development. They do curl after curl until their biceps look like cantaloupes. That's okay—if they later apply the same dedication to developing other muscles. Let's face it, a pair of 20-inch biceps looks strange alongside a scrawny chest and skinny legs. One of the goals of this book is to encourage you to develop your muscles equally—from head to toe. If you ever hope to compete in bodybuilding contests, you must be well proportioned, with no glaring weaknesses. In this chapter, we'll tell you how to develop biceps that will be the envy of others. We'll also cover the other arm muscles—the triceps and the muscles of the forearms—that sometimes get little attention. If you build these muscles as well, your biceps will appear bigger. We hope you haven't skipped the chapters on other muscle groups to get to this chapter. Arm development is essential—and fun—but it should occur at the same pace that you develop the rest of your body. With that caveat, let's talk about arms.

BICEPS

Some bodybuilders have biceps that are naturally tall, but not particularly thick and full. Others have plenty of fullness, but their biceps aren't very tall. These differences are largely the result of genetics and are hard to change At the highest levels of bodybuilding, there are few training secrets. If a top competitor realizes he needs taller biceps, he knows the exercises he must do. Still, he may not be able to achieve the height he wants. Should he become discouraged and give up? No. The biceps is one of many muscles that judges evaluate. Someone with shorter biceps may have an outstanding chest, shoulders, and legs. A bodybuilding title goes to the person with the best overall size and proportion. If you have short biceps, work hard to make them as thick and full as possible. The other dimensions can help make up for biceps that aren't tall. If you look at photographs of bodybuilding champions over the years, you'll find that not all of them had "perfect" biceps—just as they didn't all have a perfect chest, shoulders, or legs. A bodybuilding champion is the sum of the parts.

TRICEPS

Triceps, or the muscles on the back of the upper arms, are frequently overlooked. Beginning bodybuilders tend to focus on their biceps, while some may not consider exercising their triceps at all. That's unfortunate. The triceps muscle is larger than the biceps. It isn't as apparent, yet it accounts for nearly two-thirds of the size of the upper arm. As you can see, working on your triceps is the best way to improve the size of your upper arms. The triceps should have the same degree of definition as the biceps, which can be difficult to achieve. A fully developed triceps looks like an upside-down horseshoe. It has two different vertical sides as well as a thicker horizontal slab on top. It should be distinct from the deltoid muscle above it as well as from the biceps on the front of the arm. Triceps development requires dedication and commitment. Since it is a more complex muscle than the biceps, you may have to do even more exercises and sets for your triceps than for your biceps.It's impossible to hide poor triceps growth at the top levels of bodybuilding. In general, biceps exercises require bending your upper arm toward your body. Triceps workouts, on the other hand, typically call for you to straighten your upper arm against resistance. That's how you work the muscles on the back of your arms. Choose workouts that target the top, middle, and bottom of the triceps. Again, genetics plays a crucial part in the development of this muscle. Some bodybuilders may effortlessly create big triceps, whilst others must constantly "bomb" them to get similar results. In triceps exercises, hand position is crucial. A narrow grip on a barbell produces a different effect than a wide grip. With dumbbells, you get different results based on the orientation of your palms. In bodybuilding, little details can make a big difference. Be aware that some triceps exercises can cause elbow pain. Exercises that bother one person won't necessarily bother another, however, so pay attention to your elbows during and after triceps work. Don't do an exercise that is clearly painful, or you may develop a chronic problem. There are plenty of triceps exercises to choose from that likely won't cause you elbow pain.

FOREARMS

Big forearms, like big biceps, demand attention. They ensure that your lower arm is proportionate to your upper arm. Because these muscles frequently respond fast to weight training, forearm exercises can be beneficial. You can dramatically bulk up your forearms with the appropriate exercises. You'll also be able to produce stunning definition. Forearm strength is also essential. The majority of upper body exercises require forearm lifting. Other muscle groups will not benefit from the exercise if you lack the strength to lift hefty weights.

Some people incorrectly assume that they don't need to specifically train their forearms. The truth is, even though forearms are involved in most upper body exercises, these exercises don't specifically target the forearms. To achieve a well-developed physique, you must focus on each and every muscle during your training regimen. Forearms are no exception. Make them a priority right from the start.

EXERCISES

Standing Barbell Curl

Biceps

Technique: This is the most fundamental biceps workout, and it has been used by bodybuilders since the sport's inception. Kneel and grasp a barbell at shoulder width with an underhand grip (palms up, thumbs out). Straighten your arms so that the barbell rests against your thighs. Your feet should be slightly wider apart than shoulder width. Keep your body still and your elbows at your sides, then elevate your forearms (and the bar) in a wide semicircle out, up, and in toward your chest. Keep your wrists strong (do not bend them toward your torso) until the movement is complete. Stop lifting when the bar reaches the top of your chest and cannot be raised any further. Pause, then lower the barbell to the starting position, elbows at your sides.

NOTE: To get maximum benefit from this exercise, it's critical to keep your upper and lower body stationary as you lift. Wear a belt to help stabilize your lower back. Don't let your elbows move in front of your body as you lift, because that shifts some of the work from your biceps to your shoulders. If you can't keep your upper and lower body stationary while performing Curls, you're using too much weight. Proper form is more important than heavy weight. You could even injure your back if you use too much weight and sway back and forth. Advanced bodybuilders sometimes "cheat" (use their backs a little) when lifting very heavy weights. That's okay because they have years of experience and only cheat with a specific goal in mind. As a beginner, stick with strict form. For variety, you can change your grip on the bar. With a grip that's narrower than shoulder width, you'll work your inner biceps more. With a wider grip, you'll place more stress on the outer biceps.

Incline Dumbbell Curl

Technique: Sit on an incline bench. Grab a dumbbell in each hand. Let your arms hang loosely down. Keep your elbows close to your sides and slightly in front of your torso. Slowly lift both dumbbells at the same time in the regular curling motion, stopping when your arms can't go any higher. Keep your upper arms steady as you lift. At the top, pause, then lower the dumbbells to the starting position. At the bottom, stop for an extra count before lifting the dumbbells again. This will keep you from relying on momentum to swing the dumbbells up, thereby making the exercise too easy. The Incline Dumbbell Curl is also designed to minimize cheating.

NOTE: Try rotating your wrists slightly outward as you lift. Start with your palms up, then gradually rotate your wrists so that your palms are turned out at the top. As you lower the dumbbells, rotate your wrists back so that your palms are oriented up again at the bottom. Many bodybuilders find that this wrist rotation produces a higher "peak" to the biceps, as well as creating better overall size and definition.

Seated Dumbbell Curl

Technique: This exercise is identical to the Incline Dumbbell Curl, except that you sit on a flat bench. As a result, your back won't be as stable and you may have to fight a tendency to cheat. However, by sitting erect, instead of leaning against an incline bench, you work your biceps at a slightly different angle. Variety is always good in arm workouts.

NOTE: You'll get more benefit if you rotate your wrists during the movement, as described above for the Incline Dumbbell Curl. Start with your palms up, then rotate your wrists so your palms are turned out at the top. You can raise the dumbbells either one at a time or simultaneously. If you lift them one at a time, raise one arm just as the other arm reaches the lowest position; this helps create a smooth rhythm as you lift.

Hammer Curl

Technique: This exercise is identical to the Seated Dumbbell Curl, except that you start with your palms turned inward and keep them in that position throughout the movement. You don't rotate your wrists.

NOTE: By keeping your palms facing inward throughout, you work your forearm muscles as well as the biceps. You can do the Hammer Curl seated or standing. Either way, keep your elbows close to your sides and your upper arms stable. You may lift your arms either one at a time or simultaneously.

Concentration Curl

Technique: This is an excellent exercise for adding height to your biceps. Sit on the end of a flat bench with your legs apart. Grab a dumbbell in your right hand. Lean your torso forward until your back is at a 45-degree angle. Place your right elbow against the inside of your right thigh. Straighten your arm with the dumbbell near the floor. Gradually raise the weight toward your shoulder, keeping your elbow pressed against the inside of your thigh for support. At the top, pause, then lower the dumbbell to the starting position. After you finish the reps, lift with your left arm.

NOTE: When you're lifting with your right arm, place your left hand on the side of your left thigh or your forearm on top of the thigh (and vice versa). This will help keep your upper body stationary and the effort focused on your biceps. The key to this exercise is concentrating all the work on your biceps.

Triceps Cable Pressdown

Technique: Stand next to a machine with an overhead pulley and cable. Grab the horizontal bar attached to the end of the cable (it may be at eye level or slightly above your head) with an overhand grip. Place your hands 6 to 10 inches apart on the bar and your feet 6 to 10 inches apart. Hold the bar about a foot in front of your torso and even with your chest. With your elbows tucked against your sides, press down on the bar with your lower arms until it touches your thighs and your arms are straight. Keep your upper arms stable. Pause, then let the bar slowly return to a point even with your chest.

NOTE: Maintain a straight torso or a small forward lean. Don't lean so far forward that you're using your body to press down on the weights. Maintain constant cable tension while you raise and lower the weight stack. Keep your elbows parallel to your torso and do not allow them to go forward or backward. The Cable Pressdown can be performed with a variety of bars, which can be long, short, or in an inverted V shape.

Variations: There are several variations of the Cable Pressdown:

- You can use an Arm Blaster, described in the Biceps section above. This metal band rests in front of your abs and keeps your elbows in place, forcing you to do the Cable Pressdown with very strict form.

- You can lie on an incline bench, with your back to the weight stack. Grab the bar over your head and lower it into position in front of your collarbone. With this as the starting point, press down on the bar until it touches the tops of your thighs.

- You can do the Cable Pressdown with an underhand grip (palms up, thumbs out) to work the triceps from a different angle. This can be done standing or seated.

- You can press down with one arm at a time. To do this, remove the horizontal bar from the cable and replace it with a handle suitable for one hand.

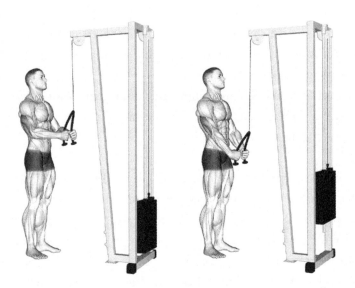

Seated Triceps Barbell Press

Technique: Sit on a flat bench and grasp a barbell in front of your chest with an overhand grip, as if you're about to press it overhead. Lift the barbell over your head and drop it till it's level with the back of your neck. Put your hands on the bar until they are barely 3 to 4 inches apart. Press the barbell up until your arms are straight overhead, with your arms bent at a 90-degree angle and your elbows on either side of your head. Maintain a firm grip on your elbows and upper arms. Return the barbell to the base of your neck.

NOTE : You can also do this exercise standing, although there's more of a tendency to cheat in that position. For variety or increased comfort, you may do this exercise with an EZ curl bar or on an incline bench.

Seated Triceps Dumbbell Press

Technique: Except for the use of dumbbells, this exercise is similar to the Seated Triceps Barbell Press. There is a wider range of motion, as with all dumbbell workouts. You can lift two dumbbells at the same time or one at a time. Hold the dumbbell(s) behind your head, palm(s) up, and bar(s) parallel to the floor. If you just have one dumbbell, you can hold it with both hands, perpendicular to the floor and palms facing inward. Raise the dumbbell(s) straight up but don't lock your elbows. Hold for a few seconds before lowering the dumbbell(s) to the starting position. As you lift, keep your elbows close to your head.

NOTE : If you lift one dumbbell at a time, place the nonlifting arm across your chest to stabilize your torso. As you lift, keep the dumbbells behind your head—not over your shoulders; this makes your triceps work harder. You may want to do the Seated Triceps Dumbbell Press in front of a mirror in order to check the position of your hands and arms. Don't use too much weight or you could injure your elbow. Perform the motion slowly, without bouncing the weight at the lowest point.

198

Dumbbell Kickback

Technique: Stand beside a flat bench. Place your left foot in front of your right. Grab a dumbbell in your left hand and bend your torso so that it's parallel to the floor. Place your right hand on the bench for support. Hold the dumbbell by your left knee, with your elbow bent at a 90-degree angle and your forearm parallel to the floor. Your palm should face inward. Keep your elbow stationary, then press the dumbbell backward until your arm is straight. The dumbbell will be behind your buttocks. Pause, then lower the dumbbell back to the starting position by your knees. When you've finished your reps, repeat the exercise with your right arm, placing your left hand on the bench.

NOTE: Don't swing the weight up. Lift it gradually, feeling your triceps at work. By using a bench for support and positioning one leg in front of the other, you should be able to isolate your triceps.

Narrow-Grip Bench Press

Technique: This exercise is identical to the regular Bench Press, except that your hands are much closer together. With Bench Press, your hands are shoulder-width apart in order to benefit your chest and shoulder muscles. To turn Bench Press into a triceps exercise, place your hands only 4 to 6 inches apart on the bar. The lifting and lowering motion is the same as with Bench Press.

NOTE: When you lift the barbell off the supports to begin the exercise, use a normal overhand grip, with your hands shoulder-width apart. This will help you more easily control and balance the bar. Once it's comfortably overhead, you can move your hands closer together, then lift and lower the barbell. For variety, you may do this exercise on an incline or decline bench. Regardless of which bench you use, keep your back firmly in place as you lift. Don't arch your back to help you lift the weight. You can also use an EZ curl bar for performing the Narrow-Grip Bench Press; this may reduce the strain on your wrists.

Triceps Machine

Technique: Most gyms have triceps machines, which are very similar to biceps machines. They typically have an adjustable seat about the height of a regular flat bench, and there may be a back to lean against. Rest your elbows on the pad. Bend your arms at the elbow so that your hands are near your face. Grab the two handles with your palms turned inward. Gradually press out and down on the handles until your arms straighten. Pause, then bend your elbows and let the handles slowly return to the starting position near your face. You should feel resistance through the entire movement.

NOTE: These machines vary widely in appearance but perform basically the same movement. They're effective because they isolate the triceps, making it harder to cheat. They also provide continuous resistance as you raise and lower the weight.

Dips

Technique: Dips were discussed earlier in this book. They are an extremely versatile exercise, but are usually thought to benefit the chest muscles. By changing your body position, however, you can work the triceps very effectively. Normally, you want to lean forward slightly as you lift and lower your body on Dips, but if you keep your torso straight up and down, the stress is shifted to your triceps. Be sure to bend your knees and cross your ankles in order to keep your legs stable. Lock your elbows at the top and lower yourself until your chest is even with the top of the bars.

NOTE: If Dips are difficult for you, don't lower yourself all the way down at first; otherwise, you risk straining your shoulders. Some dip bars have parallel horizontal bars, while others taper in at one end. If you choose the latter, experiment with different grip positions on the handlebars. Change the position of your hands on the bars to make the workout considerably more difficult once you've mastered Dips. Instead of having your palms facing inward, flip them outward. This causes your triceps to work harder when you elevate and lower your body. In addition, your chest muscles don't come into play nearly as much. However, be very careful with this reverse grip. It should only be used by advanced bodybuilders, because it places much more strain on the wrists and elbows and can therefore lead to injury. If you are uncomfortable or feel unsteady, don't do it. Go back to the normal grip, with your palms turned inward. You can attach weights to your waist for extra resistance.

Dips Behind The Back

Technique: This exercise involves doing a "dipping" motion without the use of Dip bars. Instead, two flat seats set parallel to each other and roughly 4 feet apart are used. Place your heels on one of the benches and your palms on the other. Your body will be suspended in a L form, with your legs parallel to the floor and your torso upright. Your buttocks should be directly in front of the back bench, and your arms should be straight up and down. From here, progressively bend your elbows and lower your buttocks toward the floor. As your legs angle down, keep your heels stable on the front bench. When your buttocks are a few inches off the floor, come to a halt. Don't lower yourself farther than feels comfortable. Pause, then gradually straighten your arms and raise your torso until your legs are parallel to the floor again.

NOTE: Throughout the move, keep your feet stable on the front bench. Maintain control of your body so you don't tumble to the floor unexpectedly. Dips Behind Back puts a lot of tension on your elbows, so practice it carefully. It's one of the best triceps exercises when done correctly. You can vary the placement of your hands on the bench to target different regions of the triceps. For added resistance, place a weight on your thighs or have a partner gently press down on your shoulders. However, there is no need for further resistance at first.

Forearms Wrist Curl

Technique: Place your feet shoulder-width apart on the end of a flat bench. Grab a barbell with your hands 2 to 3 inches apart and an underhand grip. Place the tops of your forearms on your thighs, angling them in slightly. The barbell and your wrists should hang slightly above your knees. Bend your wrists so that the tops of your hands are in contact with your kneecaps. The beginning point is to let the barbell roll from your palms to your fingers. Raise your wrists toward your body, maintaining your forearms pressed against your thighs. Allow the barbell to roll back onto your hands as you bend your wrists. Stop when your wrists won't go any higher. Your knuckles will be turned upward. Pause, then gradually bend your wrists down and lower the barbell again.

NOTE: Begin with light weights until you feel comfortable with this exercise. It takes practice to maintain the bar balanced when you raise and lower it with such a tiny grasp. Keep your wrists above your knees and your forearms stable throughout. You isolate your forearm muscles by moving only your wrists. Other muscles assist you when you move your entire arm. You might experiment with a wider grip on the bar for diversity. As you complete the barbell Wrist Curl, expect your forearm muscles to burn, especially at initially. That indicates that you're doing things correctly and making progress. Gradually increase the weight to avoid straining your wrists. Wrists are vital for almost all weightlifting exercises—don't risk injuring them.

Variations:

These modifications will work the forearm muscles in slightly different ways, improving their development.

Switch your grip. Instead of an underhand grip, use an overhand grip (palms down, thumbs in). Spread your hands so that they are 6 to 8 inches apart. Otherwise, repeat the Wrist Curls mentioned above. This grip places extra emphasis on the muscles on the top of your forearm. You won't be able to apply as much weight as you would with an underhand grip.

Hold the barbell behind you, against your buttocks, with your hands shoulder-width apart and palms facing away from your body. Thumbs should be pressed against the sides of your thighs. Allow the barbell to roll from your palms to your fingers in the manner described above. Your wrists will be in a straight line with your forearms at the lowest position. Then, while maintaining your forearms motionless, bend your wrists up to elevate the weight. The barbell will return to your palms.

Place your forearms on the angled armrest platform of a preacher bench. Grip a barbell overhand with your hands about 8 inches apart. Begin with your palms towards the floor and your wrists in a straight line with your forearms. Bend your wrists up and toward your body, allowing your palms to face outward.

Use dumbbells instead of a barbell. Many people prefer dumbbells for Wrist Curls because they place less strain on the wrists and they allow a longer range of motion. Sit on the end of a flat bench with your forearms on your thighs and your hands extending beyond your knees. Curl the dumbbells toward you as you would with a barbell. Start with an underhand grip, but you can also try an overhand grip. You can lift with both arms simultaneously or with one at a time.

Reverse Barbell Curl

Technique: This exercise involves your arms, not just your wrists. It is identical to the Standing Barbell Curl for biceps, except that you use an overhand grip instead of an underhand grip. That slight difference transforms it into a forearm exercise. Stand with your feet slightly more than shoulder width apart. Grab a barbell with an overhand grip and with your hands shoulder-width apart. Straighten your arms, holding the barbell against your thighs. Lift your forearms out, up, and in toward your body in a wide arc. Keep your wrists firm and your elbows at your sides. Stop when the bar almost touches your chest. Pause, then lower the weight along the same path to the starting position.

NOTE: Don't use as much weight for the Reverse Barbell Curl as you do for the Standing Barbell Curl. (Your forearm muscles are not as strong as your biceps.) Keep your upper and lower body stationary as you lift and lower the bar. Wear a belt to stabilize your lower back. Don't let your elbows move in front of or behind your torso. For variety, you can do the Reverse Barbell Curl on a preacher bench or you can use an EZ curl bar.

Reverse Cable Curl

Technique: This exercise is identical to the Reverse Barbell Curl, except that you use a machine with a floor-level pulley. With an overhand grip, hold the handle against your thighs. Lean back slightly to keep the cable taut. Then raise and lower your forearms in the same manner as described above.

Hammer Curl

Technique: We included the Hammer Curl in the biceps section, but it's equally good for forearm development. It works the upper forearm muscles where they join the biceps. Either standing or seated, hold a dumbbell at your side, with your palm turned inward and your thumb on top, and your arm hanging straight down— this is the starting position. Raise your forearm out, up, and in toward your body, stopping when you can't raise it any higher. Keep your wrist firm throughout.

Keep your elbows at your sides and your upper arms stable. You can also use a dumbbell in each hand, lifting your arms one at a time or simultaneously. If you sit, you can use a flat bench or an incline bench.

Zottman Curl

Technique: The Hammer Curl is comparable to the Zottman Curl. Hold a dumbbell in your right hand, palm up, with your arm hanging straight down. Straighten the dumbbell up toward your right shoulder. Rotate your wrist 180 degrees so that your palm is facing down about halfway up. When your right hand reaches your shoulder, come to a halt. Maintain your right elbow position. Hold for a moment, then drop the weight by turning your wrist 180 degrees back so that your palm turns up as your arm returns to your right side.

NOTE: Zottman Curls aren't commonly done today, but they're very effective for forearm development. At the beginning of the exercise, you work the muscles on the bottom of your forearm. After you rotate your wrist, your upper forearm muscles come into play. You can lift one arm at a time for several reps or you can alternate arms as you do each rep.

Leg and lower body Exercises

Beginning bodybuilders want big arms. They wouldn't mind broad shoulders and a thick chest too. And "six-pack" abs would be swell too. Unfortunately, many aspiring bodybuilders don't give any thought to their legs. Maybe they figure their legs don't show under their clothing, so why bother to develop them? Maybe they think that their thighs and calves get enough work during everyday activity and on the treadmill. Maybe they tried weight training for their legs once and thought it was too hard. Whatever the reason, avoiding leg work is a bad idea. Too often, you see people who have huge arms, massive upper bodies—and tiny legs. It looks like they've never done a leg exercise in their lives. And that may be the case.

Some people simply dislike doing leg exercises—Squats, Leg Extensions, and Leg Presses are strenuous, and even painful. It needs both mental and physical strength to persevere with them. Serious bodybuilders, on the other hand, do not avoid leg exercises because they know they cannot afford to. Today's tournaments are so competitive that well-developed legs might be the difference between winning and losing. Contestants understand that they must devote countless hours to exercising their thighs and calves. Leg training can be aggravating. Because of their genetic makeup, some people struggle to achieve large improvements, particularly in their calves. Arnold Schwarzenegger was also in this category. He claims that he never permitted his calves to be photographed when he was younger. They were so underdeveloped that he thought they would detract from the well-developed arms, shoulders, and chest that he loved to show off.

EXERCISES

Thighs Squats

Technique: Squats are the tried-and-true exercise for thigh development. They are like Bench Press for the chest and the Standing Barbell Curl for the biceps. No bodybuilding champ has ever developed his thighs without doing hours and hours of Squats. They can, however, be dangerous if done improperly. You must learn proper form before tackling even moderate weight.

To start the exercise, turn your back toward a barbell on a shoulder-height rack.(This is far safer than picking up a heavy barbell and carrying it on your shoulders.) Get under the bar by bending your knees and placing it across the back of your shoulders. Take an overhand grip with your hands somewhat wider than shoulder width apart. Make a tight grip on the bar, then straighten your legs to lift it off the rack. Take a few of steps forward. Before proceeding, ensure that the bar is appropriately balanced. Place your feet slightly wider than shoulder width apart and slightly bend your knees. Bend your knees fully and lower yourself until your thighs are slightly below parallel to the floor, keeping your back straight. At the bottom, pause and be sure you have a firm grip on the bar and a stable stance. Then gradually stand up, keeping the barbell steady on your shoulders. Don't bounce at the bottom to make standing easier. Let your thigh muscles do all the work.

NOTE: Wear a belt to protect your lower back and have a spotter nearby for further protection. It should go without saying, but before you begin, ensure sure the collars are securely fastened to the bar. You don't want weights to fall off and injure you or another person. Always maintain your head up and your eyes forward as you descend and raise yourself. This aids in the stabilization of your lower back and the prevention of injuries. Throughout the action, keep the bar directly in line with your feet. To begin, use a light weight.

With practice, you can add weight and lower yourself further—past the point when your thighs are parallel to the floor. However, do so cautiously. Some advanced bodybuilders go down so far that their buttocks touch their ankles, but this can place enormous strain on your knees and back if you're not prepared.

Variations: Squats are normally done with your feet shoulder-width apart and your toes pointing out slightly. If you widen the stance, you work your inner thighs more. If you turn your toes in, your inner thighs get even more work. A narrower stance focuses effort on the outer thighs.

Dumbbell Squat

Technique: The Dumbbell Squat is a good exercise for beginners. It involves the standard squatting motion, but you hold a dumbbell in each hand at your sides instead of having a barbell on your shoulders. With dumbbells, you don't have to worry about taking too much weight. If you do, you can simply set the dumbbells on the floor. Hold the dumbbells with your palms turned inward.

NOTE: Dumbbell Squats allow you to get used to the squatting motion. Once you gain confidence, you can move up to using a barbell or a Smith Machine. The drawback to doing this exercise with dumbbells is that you can't hold enough weight to build massive thighs.

Abdominal Exercises

Bodybuilders have long aspired to enhance their arms, chest, shoulders, and legs, but only recently have they paid attention to their abdominal muscles, sometimes known as abs. Bodybuilders today understand that a strong set of abs is just as vital as any other muscle group in winning an event. You should also pay attention to your abs as a novice. Some people associate stomach exercises with bad connotations. They recall completing endless sit-ups in gym class as children and despising them. Many different ab workouts are now available that are both more effective and more fun. Most people have a strong incentive to engage in ab exercises. After all, who doesn't want a flat, hard stomach? It's great to have broad shoulders and massive biceps, but a protruding stomach will certainly dull the impression they make. Ab exercises, done properly and faithfully, can tighten, tone, and add definition to your midsection. Genetics comes into play in developing your abs, just as it does in working your other muscles, so that some people can achieve a rock-hard, sculpted "six-pack" relatively easily. Even if you're lacking in the gene department, though, you can still improve your midsection tremendously.

It's a common myth that ab exercises alone may help you lose several inches from your waist. Despite the advertisements for some training equipment, this is known as "spot reduction," and it does not work. If you are overweight and flabby, you must change your diet and engage in a lot of aerobic exercise, such as running or riding a bike. You can tighten, firm, and flatten your tummy after losing weight. The ab workouts we'll go over aren't magic, and they won't give you washboard abs in a couple of days. They are, nevertheless, beneficial when combined with a comprehensive fitness program.

EXERCISES

Incline Board Sit-Up

Technique: Lie on your back on an incline board with your head at the bottom. Hook your feet under two roller pads that are just below the top of the board; this way, you won't slide down. Clasp your hands behind your head (fingers interlocking) with your elbows pointing outward. Raise your head slightly off the bench, then roll your shoulders and upper torso toward your knees in one motion. Stop when your torso is perpendicular to the floor and your abs are still flexed. Hold, then slowly lower yourself—but stop about 8 inches from the bench. By not going all the way down on each rep, you help avoid back problems. At the lowest point, pause, then raise your torso back to perpendicular.

NOTE: Don't bring your torso so far forward that your elbows touch your knees, for the same reason that you don't lower yourself all the way: Both can cause back pain or injury. All the benefit to your abs comes in the middle part of the motion. Don't raise your torso abruptly on the first rep. Raise and lower yourself gradually and under control. To make the Incline Board Sit-Up more difficult and more effective, twist your torso slightly in either direction as you bring your torso forward. Turn a little to the left on one rep, so your right elbow points at your left knee. On the next rep, do the reverse. This way, you work the intercostal muscles at the top and sides of your abs. For variety, you can hold a light weight behind your head to add resistance. If you find this exercise painful, skip it. There are other abdominal exercises that are just as effective.

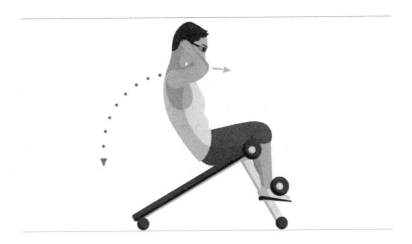

Crunches

Technique: Crunches are a very effective ab exercise with several variations. For the basic crunch, lie on the floor with a flat bench crosswise in front of you. Rest the backs of your calves and ankles on the bench, with your legs bent at a 90-degree angle. Clasp your hands behind your head (fingers interlocking), raise your head slightly off the floor, then roll your shoulders toward your knees a few inches. Don't lift your back off the floor; this can cause injury, and it doesn't benefit your abs. As you raise yourself, "crunch"—or flex—your abs.

NOTE: As alternatives, you can cross your arms across your chest instead of clasping your hands behind your head or you can twist from side to side as you sit up. Do each rep slowly and deliberately. You should be able to feel your abs contracting and strengthening. Don't thrust your shoulders forward on the way up.

Twists

Technique: This exercise uses no weights—only a long bar (or broom handle). Sit on the end of a flat bench with your feet on the floor. Place the bar behind your head, resting it across the back of your shoulders, and hold it. Keeping your head still and your eyes looking forward, bend your torso to the right as far as possible. Your shoulders should rotate at about a 90-degree angle so that they're turned sideways. Hold, then rotate in the opposite direction.

NOTE: You want a slow, deliberate motion to work the abs. Be careful not to swing your torso from side to side. Keep your buttocks and thighs firmly on the bench—don't let them lift up. For variety, you can stand and perform the same movement, with your feet slightly more than shoulder-width apart. You can also bend forward from the waist so that your torso is almost parallel to the floor, then twist from side to side. As you do, keep your head down and your eyes looking at the floor in front of your feet. Do the motion under control. Twisting movements— whether standing or seated—develop the intercostal muscles at the top and sides of your abs. Twists are also an excellent warm-up exercise at the beginning of your workout because they loosen up the entire upper body. You can hold a bar with an overhand grip using your fingers or you can place your wrists and lower forearms on top of the bar to support it.

Cardiovascular Exercises for beginners

Bodybuilders want to bulk up, but they might get so focused on muscle growth that they overlook another vital aspect of fitness: cardiovascular conditioning. Cardiovascular exercise, such as running or biking, increases lung capacity and endurance. It is also beneficial at the gym. If you're in better cardiovascular fitness, you can work out with weights for longer and harder, which is a significant bonus. After all, performing many sets of heavy weight is highly exhausting, so you'll need all the endurance you can get. Ignoring cardio, or aerobic, work is incredibly unwise. If you do, you may be limiting your ability to grow muscle. We're not talking about doing hours and hours of aerobic exercise. As a general rule, about 30 minutes of cardio work three or four times a week is a good start, as long as you're disciplined about it. It's always easy to convince yourself that you need to take it easy or spend more time in the gym instead.

Many bodybuilders approach cardiovascular training in the same way they approach ab and leg work. They believe you're wasting your time because you can't see a healthy heart and lungs. Aside from increasing endurance, aerobic exercise offers another advantage. It burns fat significantly more effectively than lifting weights. Running, riding, swimming, or any other sort of cardio exercise you choose will result in higher muscle definition if your body has less fat. If you incorporate aerobic exercise into your routine early on, you're more likely to continue with it in the long run—and reap the benefits. On days when they don't lift, most bodybuilders engage in cardio exercise. This makes sense.

If you try to do strenuous aerobics after a hard lifting session, you'll be too exhausted to see effects. Similarly, if you begin your weight training with intense cardio, you will become weary and your lifting will suffer. Light cardio exercise, on the other hand, is beneficial at the start of your weightlifting sessions.

Five or ten minutes on a stationary bike, for example, can get your heart thumping, your blood flowing, and your muscles flexible, preparing your body for an intense workout. The more you warm up, the less likely it is that you will strain a muscle. A little aerobics might also be beneficial at the end of a strenuous weight-lifting session. It'll help you gradually wind down, reflect on your lifting, and make mental notes for your next workout. It's easier on your body to gradually reduce the intensity of your workout than to go full bore and then stop suddenly. In addition, cardio exercise can actually tone your muscles and help them recover from a grueling weight session.

In addition, most gyms feature other cardiovascular equipment. There are stair devices, for example, that allow you to "climb" stairs in position. In recent years, "elliptical" machines have gained popularity, simulating a running action while providing an impact-free workout. On these machines, you stand upright and set your feet on two oval surfaces slightly larger than your shoes, then you start "running," and the platforms move in a lengthy, elliptical course that simulates running.

Swimming is another excellent aerobic exercise. It's very demanding, and it can produce excellent results in a short amount of time, particularly if you aren't accustomed to swimming. If you haven't been swimming in a while, it may take some time to get in the groove. As you can imagine, swimming is easy on the joints. It can also be enjoyable and relaxing. Even if you don't like to swim, you can still get a good workout in the pool by running. That may sound odd, but running in 3 or 4 feet of water provides excellent resistance and gives you a great low-impact workout. You'll be surprised at how difficult it is—you certainly won't make great time. However, your heart, lungs, and leg muscles will definitely feel the results. Running, biking, and swimming are the most common forms of cardio exercise, but there are many more. Hiking, jumping rope, playing tennis, softball, or golf (if you walk rather than ride in a golf cart) all provide good cardio benefits.

You can appreciate other activities that provide a solid cardio workout.

Most elite bodybuilders work out with cardio all year, but some may do less during the "off season" when they aren't training for a competition. They're normally seeking to develop muscular mass during this time, but they also want to keep their heart and lungs in good shape. Bodybuilders typically boost their aerobic training dramatically in the weeks leading up to a competition in order to lose fat and improve muscle definition.

We should also mention that it's possible to do too much cardio work. Particularly when you're in intense training, you shouldn't do lengthy, demanding aerobics—such as running long distances on a regular basis—because if you do, you'll tax your body too much. Weight training requires tremendous stamina and strength, and if your body is weak from miles of running, you won't get the full benefit in the gym. Remember— your goal is to become a bodybuilder, not a marathon runner. A cardio program should always complement your weight training, not detract from it. Excessive cardio work can also make it difficult to retain muscle mass. If you are thin by nature, you may already have trouble gaining quality weight. If you add in too much cardio, you can sweat off your muscle as well as your fat. Be smart, and pay attention to your progress. Everyone, no matter how thin, needs to do some aerobics in order to strengthen the cardiovascular system and build endurance. Bodybuilders who have a tendency to get too heavy may always need to do more aerobics than thinner people. Everyone is different. Success in bodybuilding depends on customizing both your weight training and your aerobics program for your physique.

Made in the USA
Middletown, DE
30 November 2023

44100728R00126